He Wrapped My Pain In His Glory

Apostle Dr. Muriel & Co-Pastor Danny Fuqua
Word And Praise Family Church, Inc.
955 Orange Avenue, Suite 120
Daytona Beach, Florida 32114

(386) 257-2559 www.wordandpraisefamilychurch.org

(386) 492-5493 www.mfuquaministries.org

Printed in the United States of America

First Printing, 2014

ISBN: 150070704X

Ordering Information:
Order by contacting the author at the above listed information.
ISBN 13: 9781500707040
Library of Congress Control Number: 2014913917
CreateSpace Independent Publishing Platform, North Charleston, SC

DEDICATION

This book is dedicated to the individuals who have been wounded and injured spiritually and are having difficulties in being made whole again. It is also dedicated to those whom God appointed as spiritual surgeons to assist the wounded and injured spirits.

A SPECIAL THANKS

First, I thank my best friend, my lover, my companion, and my king, Pastor Danny Fuqua, for being the man of God that he is, and for supporting me through the process of completing this book. He is the wind beneath my wings. I also thank the fruit of my womb, Phebe and Daniel, and my son-in-law Jimmy, for being by my side. I thank my grandchildren Amaziah, Jaylisa, and Hezekiah for giving me daily hope, just by looking at their joyful faces and their daily growth. I am thankful that the birth of all three of them gave me continuous hope of the healing and miraculous power of God. I praise God daily for my dear friend and covenant sister, Pastor Essina Robinson, for allowing God to use the surgical anointing He gave me to help her during some of her toughest and most trying times, and for being one of my prayer partners, a confidant, and a true God-given forever friend. To my Goddaughter and armor bearer, Minister Susan Lewis, who never gave up on my vision, and who spent countless nights praying for me and going into constant warfare for me, my marriage, my family, and the church. Our relationship is like none other. To my dear first cousin, Evangelist Gail Goss, who always supported me and caused me to always remain humble, as she expressed to everyone these words: "Dr. Fuqua is my shero." (hero). To my dear friend, Minister Vanessa Trimble, for spending hours editing and proofreading my book, and for always being there to encourage and assist me in anything I needed. I love you, Nessa. To all of the members of Word And

Praise Family Church, Inc. who believed in the Jesus in their Pastors, and supported the vision that God has given us: to reach, restore, revive, and release people to impact the world for Jesus Christ, and for all of the WPFC I.N.S.P.I.R.E. covenant members and partners, who financially supported the publishing of this book. To my brilliant brother, Mr. Lanzio Jordan, who passionately edited my book, and gave me advice from his experiences in psychology and from counseling so many youth and adults. I love him more than words can express. To my friend and co-worker, Professor Sandra Offiah-Hawkins, for being there for me during some of my toughest days. Sandra, thank you for all of the long days and nights of editing my book. Thank you for believing in my dreams of helping and touching the lives of God's people. To Apostle Mary Brinson-McMiller, for helping me with the initial publishing and editing of my book. I appreciate you for the jump-start and the encouragement to go ahead and publish my book. To all, whose names I did not mention, who helped me through my life's journey, I thank you. I love all of you, and the best is yet to come!

Table of Contents

Foreword

PASTOR DANNY FUQUA

When my wife Muriel first asked me to write a fore-word to her book, I knew that her book would not be complete without my being able to express my feelings to her, by letting her know that I support the mission that she is on. Nothing was more disturbing and painful than the day when my wife asked me if it was something that I needed to tell her and talk to her about. My word to other men is this: *"If you are dealing with the dark side of your life and are not faithful to your spouse, it is not worth it."* Come to the light: A true relationship with Jesus Christ. I say to the men who are facing the same challenges that I faced in life: *Own up to your responsibility and be truthful and faithful to your spouse. You can only run so far and live in the darkness of life for so long.*

When I was confronted by my wife about my past, I knew it was time to stop running and face my challenges and the life I was living. It was not easy, but it was well worth it. Since I have renewed my relationship with my wife and with God, it is like the darkness has gone away, and the light has come on. It was not something that happened overnight, but by seeking coun-seling and seeking forgiveness, the light officially and eventu-ally came on. Every morning and every day was a struggle, dealing with the embarrassment and shame that I bought to my family. It is a path that I never want to travel ever again.

It was a path that was very unpleasant, restless, stressful, and uncomfortable.

Men, we are to value our wife and family. We must cherish them as a precious jewel. If you lose a jewel in the natural, it can be symbolic of losing the family that is very, very special to you. If you are dealing with the dark side of life, I ask that you seek God for forgiveness. Ask your family for forgiveness, and *turn right and go straight.* You may think to yourself that it is not something that is easy to do, and honestly, it's not. But with God, all things are possible. My wife is my best friend, my queen, my lover, and my companion. She was the one who kept our family together during the tough times of our lives. Without her being a forgiving wife, our marriage would have ended. I am grateful to have a wife who is willing to hear God and obey His will. I am also grateful that we serve a God of a second chance. We serve a forgiving God. Many men and women who have walked and lived in darkness were offered the opportunity of a second chance, and did not use or accept the chance. I am grateful to have my family that stood beside me and my wife during the hardest times of our lives.

Both my wife and I will use the trials, tribulations, our encounters with abuse, and the love we have for each other, to reach and restore people to impact the world for Jesus Christ. There are so many hurting people who have experienced many horrible things in life that caused their sexual habits to become a dysfunctional lifestyle. When those experiences take place, they become a major distraction, and hinders the person from focusing on the will of God for his or her life. Our mission is to help people who are facing the same challenges in life that we faced. Sometimes we may not understand why we were victims, and why things such as sexual abuse happened to us in life; therefore, we go for many years living with the shame and embarrassment of our past, regretting the things that happened to us, that were really beyond our control. However, if we as parents, pastors, spiritual leaders, teachers, coaches, and those with other leadership roles en-force the open communication that it is *'okay'* to tell someone that we have been abused, it will change lives forever. A cycle will be broken, and a repeat of sexual abuse will not be carried on to the next generation.

My wife and I will touch many lives by taking a stand, and preaching the true gospel of Jesus Christ, and being available for other couples who are facing the dark side of life that we went through, and are willing to make a change. We will not only be available to couples, but for single individuals as well. My wife and I will use the trials, tribulations, our encounters with abuse and pain, and the love we have for each other, to touch the lives of many people who want to experience true freedom.

Chapter 1

The Ribbon of Abuse

I have often preached about my disturbing, shattering, and demoralizing years of incest, but putting it in a book has been my desire for many years. My memory of abuse goes as far back as I can remember, which is about the age of five. That abuse was mainly mental and emotional abuse from seeing my father cruelly and ruthlessly beat my mother for no reason at all, day in and day out. The only cologne that I can recall from my dad was his whisky smelling breath. My dad was an alcoholic, and upon arriving home from work, he would immense to slamming doors and calling my mother names that scared her for life. He would throw her between the small white oven in our miniature size kitchen, and she would lie on the floor appearing to be lifeless. As I watched the horrible sight, I would ball into a knot, crying, *"Leave her alone! No! Stop!"* The fiery tears rolling from my face felt like heat, and the heat was the burning hatred in my heart toward my father. The fetal position that I was in stitched the seams of the ribbon of abuse that would consequently spiral out of control. I hated my dad for beating my mother like that, and I vowed that a man would never beat me.

I remember vividly when my mother decided that enough was enough. She packed our clothes and gathered our suitcases. My dad was at work. She took us to the nearest bus station.

We were headed for my grandmother's house in Mississippi. From this point in my life, the ribbon of abuse took a spiral turn. Even though the mental and emotional abuse from my father taunted me a great period of my life, I believe the abuse that taunted me the most was the sexual abuse from other relatives. That abuse came to me in the form of incest. *Incest* is something the church does not talk much about. For years, it has been *a "hush-hush"* topic in the church, and that is why there were (and still is) so many devastated, depressed, and downtrodden women and men in the church. These people go through life desiring to be delivered from their past of the dreadful generational curse of *incest,* but they are afraid. They were told that it was *a family secret* that should never be talked about, or discussed with anyone.

I am confident this is why God prompted me to put my life's story in a book, so others could be healed and delivered from their past of pain and devastation. When people read my story, they will see that they weren't the only ones targeted by the demons of *incest.* They will understand why they didn't lose their mind, and they will know how they have survived incest for so long. After reading this book, they will know that it was the Glory of God that was over their lives.

My first memory of being sexually abused was when I was around ten or eleven years old. A male first cousin of mine, who was 11 years older than I, convinced me to go into what we called *"the back room"* with him. The back room was our Grandpa's room, and none of the children were allowed to go back there. It was because of Grandpa's two jobs. He was what we called *"the store."* He sold moon pies, potato chips, soda pops, freezer pops, and all kinds of goodies. And, the back room was where his goodies were stored. And for a lack of a better word, Grandpa was also *"the moon shine man."* Now, he didn't actually make all of the liquor he sold, but he did sell liquor. Where he got it all, to this day, I don't really know.

But in my mind's eye, I can see him now, limping on one leg, with a walking stick in one hand, and a small brown bag in his other hand, (tucked under his thigh) as he walked from the back room. There was one occasion when talking with him, he told me and some other cousins that he would show us how to make moon shine. I was fascinated, and told him to show us how. When he verbally gave the ingredients, I assured him that I could make the best moon shine ever, and everyone would buy it. He laughed, and thought I was joking. With his permission, I gathered the ingredients and went to work.

After long hours of brewing my prized possession, it was time for a taste test. Grandpa tasted my drink, and laughed until he cried. *"Girl, what is this? This is not moonshine! This is grape juice!"* During that time, a white man would come by in a white van selling Grandpa's store items. His name was Mr. Coffee. I told him I was going to sell my whiskey to him, for some potato chips. Surely enough, Mr. Coffee came by, tasted my whiskey, and laughed like Grandpa. Regardless of the laughs, I still got my potato chips (plus some popcorn), but I eventually gave up on the moonshine business.

Since the backroom was a private place, where else would my male first cousin try to take me for his nasty, offensive, sexual behaviors? The back room was the perfect place. And it was in this back room that I was forced to have sex with him. It was at that point that my inadequate grape juice concoction seemed pointless and less rewarding. All of my inner innocence and virginity were stolen from me. My trust was broken, and the seam in the ribbon of pain and abuse grew increasingly longer. I felt scared, ashamed, and nasty, and those dreadful feelings followed me most of my adult life.

After the first incident of incest, it seemed that the word got out to every male cousin I had, and one after another, day after day, they would manipulate me for years, raping me of my innocence. The most horrible memory occurred when I was around eleven, or twelve. I remember playing, having fun, and enjoying being a kid, when another male cousin took me on the *back porch* near the *"back room."* Boy, it's something about those back places. The back places were dangerous and life changing for me. The enemy uses *back places* to try to "steal, kill, and destroy."

It was on the back porch that I felt the lowest. My male cousin was forcing his penis in me (which hurt terribly), and I kept telling him, *"No, I don't want to do this. It hurts. Someone is going to catch us."* The prophetic gifting must have been activated and working overtime within me that day, because just as sure as I predicted, we were caught having sex. Yes, on that morbid, dark, gruesome day, my grandmother caught us having sex. To my surprise, she started to yell things that caused me to experience even more mental and emotional distress. This pain lasted until my late adult life. She yelled, *"What y'all doing! Gal get yo fast tail in the house! You nasty fast tail gale!"* Gone *boy...get yourself away from here! I'm going to tell your Mama on your fast tail self."* Then, my grandmother commenced to beat me, as I ran frightfully into the house. I felt paralyzed. I thought my grandmother would hold me, and tell me she was sorry that my older cousin was doing such a horrible thing to me, but she didn't. Instead, she blamed me. That happened early in the day, and all day long, I was worried about what my mother was going to do to me when she came home from work. Besides, my mother was my grandmother's daughter. Would she do the same thing that my grandmother did to me? Would she beat me also? Would she call me awful, dreadful names too? All of those questions rushed through my little confused, chaotic mind.

To make my life even more miserable, my grandmother proceeded to tell my male cousin's mom what had happened. Then the both of them began criticizing me, telling me that I made him do that to me, because I was what they called "fast." In rural Mississippi, the expression "fast, tail girl" referred to a girl who was promiscuous. Now, I was far from being a promiscuous little girl. Therefore, that comment took me further into the hole of pain and despair. I felt like the whole world was ending. Some hours later, both my grandmother and aunt called me into the house and asked, *"Do you want us to tell your momma?"* Since I didn't know what my mother was going to do, obviously I said, *"No..."* Their response afterwards was, *"Well, you had better be obedient, and do whatever we tell you, from now on."* Truthfully, the hurting little girl really wanted her mother to know. She wanted her mother to tell her that it was not her fault. That day began my life of being blackmailed into being what most of my cousins knew me as, *"a good girl."* At this point in my life, the ribbon of abuse had grown so long until it felt like it was choking me.

A few years later (at the age of 14 – March 16, 1977), I finally heard the voice of the Lord, and gave my life totally to God. I had been seeking God to come into my heart, but on that day, I received the baptism of the Holy Ghost, and began to speak in tongues as the spirit of God gave me utterance. At that time, I was the only young person in our entire church that had totally given their life to God. I was, (as people in our church called it) the only *"saved, sanctified, and Holy Ghost filled young person in the church."*

Now, in my hometown, there was a *"reverence"* for anyone who said that they were *"saved,"* or had *"given their life to God."* From that time on, salvation became my refuge for not being molested anymore. Instead of being pulled into *the back room*, immediately, if another cousin saw a male cousin trying to bother me, he would say, *"Man, you had better stop! That girl is saved!"* I had gone from the *back room* to the *Upper Room*! Glory to God! I thank God for Salvation! It was salvation and the Glory of God that kept me from being molested! That ribbon of abuse was dipped in the blood of Jesus, and I finally felt a sense of hope, and purpose in my life.

Yes, I really did love Jesus at the early age of 14, but I believe I loved the freedom of my body not being abused anymore the most. And would you know, *"Even though I was saved, that did not stop the blackmail from my grandmother and aunt."* Every now and then, my grandmother would ask me, *"You remember what you did with ####?"* And even though I was a grown woman, the shame that the little girl felt, would flood through my entire body and soul, like a tsunami. Most of the times, I did not even respond to the question. I can only remember my aunt asking me once, a few years after the incident. Trauma has a way of making you suppress things, so I can't recall any other occasions of her asking me.

It was God's Glory that kept me. He literally wrapped my pain in His Glory. I constantly prayed and stayed in God's presence. I constantly read the Bible. God would show me visions and visit me in my dreams. His Glory assured me daily that He was there to protect me from harm, danger, and any more pain of that sort.

For years I did not hate my grandmother and aunt, but I always wondered why they treated me in such a wrongful way. Both of them did great things for me, like giving me money and gifts, when others didn't get any gifts or money. Therefore, most of my relatives saw me as *"the family's favorite."* But I knew the real truth. I knew the family secrets. And deep in my heart, I knew the things that had happened to me were not my fault. I knew I had been forced to have sex for years with so many cousins. My childhood for years was a constant manhunt, running from one male cousin, to another male cousin. This book is only giving a snippet of the many male figures that taunted me year in and year out. While growing up in Mississippi, my life was such a constant nightmare, that to this day, I rarely go back to my hometown to visit. If I do, it's normally for a funeral, or the death of a close relative. I have gone there to do a crusade, but that's about it.

Despite the numerous years of pain, I am grateful that God always gives a closure to pain. Many, many years later, I remember visiting my grandmother (She must have been in her early seventies). She asked me that same question: *"Muriel, do you remember what you did with #####?"* You will have to understand the state of mind that my grandmother was in, to really get an idea of what I was feeling. She was in the early stages of dementia. So, she was in and out of her *"right (sane) mind."* But even though I felt that same old nasty, cold feeling, what she said afterwards (for the first time) began to make that nasty, cold feeling melt away. She said, *"Baby, I'm sorry. Grandmamma was wrong. Will you forgive me? Do you forgive me?"* My reply was, *"Grandma, I forgive you."* At that moment, I had so much love for my grandmother, until nothing else really mattered. She really didn't mean to hurt me. After digging into God's Word, and learning about generational curses, I later found out that molestation, sexual abuse, and a promiscuous lifestyle was a part of my family's unfortunate heritage. It was a bloodline curse that needed to be broken and destroyed. Wow, what a heritage to leave another generation!

I still needed something else. The little girl (that was trapped inside my adult body) still wanted her mother to know what had happened to her. Years later, after my mother moved to Florida, I wrote her a long letter, and gave vivid details about my years of molestation. I gave her names, and I told her about the years of being blackmailed. She was confounded beyond words. After I told her, she just sadly asked, *"Baby, why didn't you tell Momma? Why?"*

Not only did I tell my Momma, but I also was able to write that first male cousin a long letter. I expressed to him how he had hurt me severely, and learned later that life had dealt him that same deck of *incest* and *molestation cards.* Hurting people, hurt people. But this book will reveal to you how *healed people, heal people.* I am writing this book so that thousands of people can be healed from any type of pain they have experienced.

After that family secret got out, other female and male cousins came forth and told their stories. Just like me, they too

11

had been trapped by the demons of incest and molestation. It was a dreadful cycle that needed to be broken. Of course we got through those rough times, because when truth is revealed, the devil is angry. His anger causes others to say and do things that are ungodly. It's not easy bringing skeletons and secrets out of the family closet. A lot of hearts were broken and a lot of tears were shed. But, great healing took place. I give credit for all of the healing to God's Glory. I am certain after reading this book, many more hearts will be hurting from the family secrets being revealed, but I am also even more confident that many hearts will be healed by God's radiant Glory!

The Glory of God is fascinating. It was God's Glory that allowed me to tell one of my cousins that I forgave him, and I began ministering to him, and prophesying into his life. It was God's Glory that drew my family closer and closer together. It was God's Glory that took our pain away. I am certain that God will take your pain away also, and wrap all of your pain in His Glory, just like He did for me.

I have never confronted any of the other cousins (not even the one that Grandmamma caught me with). I often wondered why. One reason could be because shortly after the incident, he moved away, and I did not know his whereabouts. Eventually, the Holy Spirit told me that it was not necessary to talk with him. God let me know that He needed me to deal with the "genesis" of the incest and molestation seed that was planted in me. That seed was from the first cousin. After I dealt with that initial incest incident, year after year, God continued to wrap all of my pain in His Glory.

If you are reading this chapter, and you have experienced the sickening, dreadful, trauma of being molested by a relative through the generational curse of incest, do know that God can wrap all of that hurt and pain in His Glory. You have to allow Him to transform your pity into praise, and your sorrow into joy. Let His Glory transform you from a victim to a victor. Let Him take your mess and transform it into a message. Use your story to help get someone else full deliverance. Let God wrap all of your pain in His *"Glory."* Finally, read this prayer aloud:

"Father, in the Name of Jesus, I thank you for another opportunity to trust Your Word. Lord, you told me to call upon you in the time of trouble. Help me. And Father God, by the power vested in the name of Jesus Christ, I BIND THE satanic FORCES OF CHILD ABUSE, INCEST, MOLESTATION, AND CHILD PORNOGRAPHY that is at work in my family, and even in this nation. God, I realize that the devil does not play fair, and what has happened to me and my family is not my fault. I understand that the devil comes to steal, kill, and destroy, but Jesus, You have come to give me and my family life, and life more abundantly. God, I come against every assignment of the devil, and I call all of his assignments null and void. And right now, I loose the spirit of complete healing within me and my entire family. Father, help those who hurt me. And God, continue to wrap my pain in Your Glory. In Jesus' Name I pray, Amen."

Chapter 2

WE NEED GOD'S GLORY

I couldn't have survived any of my life's pain and trauma, without the Glory of God. And the main element for spiritual growth that is lacking in the lives of God's people is *God's Glory*. The word 'glory' is used often in churches all across this world, but sadly, there are so many Christians who do not know what the real Glory of God is. They also do not know the relevancy of God's Glory in the life of the believer. God wants every human being to experience His Glory. The Glory of God is His splendor, beauty, power, wonder, dignity, and His awe. It is the revelation of God's Glory that is going to equip the Church for the perilous times that we now live in. *II Timothy 3:1* tells us about these times. *"This know also, that in the last days perilous (dangerous; unsafe) times shall come."* We are in those dangerous, unsafe times right now, and that is why we as believers need to experience the Glory of God in our lives. God has commissioned me to share with the world how *He can wrap any of life's pains in His Glory.*

When the word *pain* is used, most people think only of physical pain from an illness. When I refer to *pain* in this book, you will see how God's Glory healed me from pain that I incurred *physically, emotionally, spiritually, mentally, socially, intellectually, and economically.* As you continue to read about my life's experiences, my testimonies will show you what the Glory of God can do with any type of pain you may suffer, and how to use your pain to rescue others from their past discomforts, tragedies, distress, and agony.

There was an illustration in the scriptures where Moses wanted to experience God's glory. Exodus 33:18-23 reads, *"¹⁸And he said, I beseech thee, shew me thy glory. ¹⁹And he said, I will make all my goodness pass before thee, and I will proclaim the name of the LORD before thee; and will be gracious to whom I will be gracious, and will shew mercy on whom I will shew mercy. ²⁰And he said, Thou canst not see my face: for there shall no man see me, and live. ²¹And the LORD said, Behold, there is a place by me, and thou shalt stand upon a rock: ²²And it shall come to pass, while my glory passeth by, that I will put thee in a cleft of the rock, and will cover thee with my hand while I pass by: ²³And I will take away mine hand, and thou shalt see my back parts: but my face shall not be seen."*

Many times when people think of the Glory of God, they only think of a physical manifestation. As humans we tend to be very fleshy or carnal, and base life only on our five senses. For some people, God's Glory is only seen through their eyes when they think of the creation of the world, or when they receive enormous material blessings (money, homes, or cars). Others may walk on the ocean and see the beauty of the waters and the waves, and grasp this as God's Glory. Some may stand on a mountain peak and view the valleys that have formed below and perceive this as God's Glory. Others only look at their material, substantial income and perceive this as God's Glory. Consequently, these people tend to put their *presents* (gifts) from God on a higher scale than God's actual *presence* (His Glory).

At other times the Glory of God could be an ecstatic feeling that overcomes us, like chills throughout our body, and tears running down our cheeks. Then, there is the spontaneous running or unexplained shouting that many do, in the edifice of a church. Frequently people feel that if they go to church and not cry, shout, and run and dance across the floor that God's Glory is not in the church. That is far from truth. The Glory of God can even be a distinctive atmosphere or a luminous radiation. You can be in a room, and suddenly there is a stillness or even a bright light or glow surrounding the entire place. You can rub your eyes and try to wipe away the glow, but it still remains in the room. There have been times when rooms and churches have been filled with smoke, or a fog. When this happens, you sense or feel that someone or something is in the room, other than the person or people who can be physically seen. You sense a supernatural presence. That light, glow, or sense of someone or something being there is often the Glory of God. It is often God's very presence.

I have learned from my pain (all of the types that I mentioned earlier) that the greatest form of God's glory *is the revelation of His nature and attributes*. You see, more than anything else I have experienced in life, it was my pain that taught me more about God's divine characteristics and power. It was my pain that taught me the real essence of God's Glory. As I went through various stages of pain, God walked me through the process of growing *from the milk of who He really is*, to *the meat of His nature*. During my milk stage (just as with a baby), I reacted to pain like a child. But as I matured in God and learned more about His Glory, I moved from the milk of God to the meat of knowing Him. When we learn God's nature and attributes, we also gain a greater relationship with God. We begin to be more like Him in every aspect of our lives. When we become more like Him, He literally *wraps our pain in His Glory*.

I remember praying the prayer that Moses prayed. I said, *"Lord, show me your glory."* When we pray, *"Lord show me your glory,"* we are actually saying, *"Lord, reveal to me who you are, and what my purpose in life is, while I am on planet earth. What do you want to do with me? How should I handle all of the pain I am experiencing?"* Whether you know it or not, as long as you live on this earth, you will experience some type of pain.

In order to know who God is, we must grow in the knowledge of God. I learned later in life that during the times I
stayed on the milk too long, my pains intensified. I had to
learn what Paul was talking about in I Corinthians 3:1-2. *"And
I, brethren, could not speak unto you as unto spiritual, but as unto
carnal, even as unto babes in Christ. (2) I have fed you with milk, and
not with meat: for hitherto ye were not able to bear it, neither yet now
are ye able."* I had to learn the importance of growing in the
knowledge of God.

The word *'grow'* means *to produce, to cultivate, to raise, to develop, to expand, or to increase.* Many times we cannot produce,
cultivate, raise, develop, expand, or increase in God, because
of the pain that has occurred in our lives. If we are on the
same spiritual level that we were on, last year, we need to examine our *"pain level."* If we are in the same place in God that
we were in when we first accepted Jesus into our lives, we need
to examine our *"pain level."* Most people do not know how to
examine their pain level. One way my pain level was examined
was with the relationship I had with my father.

From a young child, all the way through my young adult
life, my pain level was very high. In saying that, I mean the way
pain had affected me. I experienced great *mental* and *emotional*
pain from my father. He would curse my mother out for no
reason. He would slap her, beat her, and call her everything
but a child of God. Daily hearing this abuse caused my pain
level to be *high,* (meaning almost unbearable) not only when
my Dad did those things, but when I heard others being inflicted with that type of pain. I vividly remember flinching
when I heard profanity, and my insides would ball into a fetal
position when I would see others mentally and emotionally
abused. As I learned more about God's Glory, the bar of my
pain level was *lowered,* which allowed me to react differently
when that type of pain was inflicted upon me, or when it was
inflicted upon others. This had a lot to do with my *healing*

level. As I grew in the knowledge of God, when pain was felt again, I reacted with less distress and anguish.

After examining our pain *levels*, we need to examine our *"levels of healing."* When we grow in the knowledge of God, our pain will pull out the best that is on the inside of us. Pain produces growth, and growth brings stability to our lives. The relationship with my father, and men in general, was not stable until my healing level was raised. When I began to understand who God really was in my life, God's Glory wrapped the mental and emotional pain incurred from my father, inside of His Glory. Therefore, I did not react or feel the pain like I used to. When the pain level was *high* I hated my father, and I thought most men were like him. When the pain level was *lowered* (because I matured in the knowledge of God), I began to love my father, and pray for his weaknesses.

Remembering the mental and emotional pain from my father, reminded me of the process of our spiritual growth and maturity as Christians. I compare it to the times when I was raising my children. There were many wonderful and exciting moments that I can clearly remember. The intensified emotional moments were probably the actual birth of my children and the times when they said their first words, or when they started crawling, walking, and talking, and doing things in the ministry. When I saw these various stages of progression in my children's life, I was happy and thrilled about what life would bring to them, on the next level of their growth. Each level of their growth meant *maturity.* The falls, cuts, burns, and scraps helped them to grow. It helped them to understand what to do, and what not to do. Not only was I excited about my children's progression, but I would often observe their excitement, when they saw their own growth.

What I have noticed in the Body of Christ is less excitement about *"progression and growth."* Spiritually, many believers are in a continuous crawling stage, and they look very strange. It's sad, but I believe a lot of them love *"the spiritual baby stage,"* because of the need for *"attention."* They enjoy others picking them up, and rubbing and kissing their little "boo boos." Often it is because they did not receive hugs and kisses when they were children. Therefore, they bring this same baby mentality into the church.

My children would look very strange today (as adults) if they were yet crawling and sucking a bottle. Something would be terribly wrong! I would have had to take them to a Specialist a long time ago, for extensive testing! If we are continuously crawling spiritually, we need to go to the Specialist! We need to go to God, and seek more of His Glory! We need to seek Jesus! Living for Christ should be a process of *growing from Glory to Glory.* We cannot progress in God effectively, if we don't allow Him to *"wrap our pain in His Glory."*

What many believers fail to realize is the fact that *"There is a price to pay in order to receive God's Glory!"* Just like the Biblical woman with the alabaster box, there is a high price for *the oil of the anointing.* The anointing is the yoke destroying, burden removing power of the living God, that He has placed on the inside of every born again believer.

So many Christians tend to forget the foundational things of God, and forget about the value of their anointing. When we first received Christ in our lives, we had to seek God. Matthew 6:33 says, *"But seek ye first the kingdom of God, and his righteousness; and all these things shall be added unto you."* The word "seek" means *to pursue, run after,* or *to even stalk God.* When we pursue God, He will flood us with His Glory. Additionally, He will wrap all of our pain in His Glory. When we don't seek God (and seek other things) life's pains will try to consume and destroy us. When that occurs, we tend to wrap our pain in our circumstances. The motive of the thief (the devil) is to steal, kill, and destroy. But Jesus has promised us as Christian believers, life and life more abundantly.

When we seek God, we cannot help but "reverence the holiness of God." Psalms 30:4 says, *"Sing unto the Lord, O ye saints of his, and give thanks at the remembrance of his holiness."* When we truly seek God, worship will become our lifestyle. When it does, our pain will literally be wrapped in *the Glory of God.*

When worship becomes a lifestyle, we will also *"have a heart of repentance."* We will forgive those who caused us to have pain in our lives. Acts 3:19 says, *"Repent ye therefore, and be converted, that your sins may be blotted out, when the times of refreshing shall come from the presence of the Lord."* My forgiveness will be talked about in other chapters. To repent means *to change, turn away from, or turn around.* The Glory of God will give such a turn-around in your life until you won't even feel the effects of pain. Actually, God will give you a time of amnesia, and allow you to forget the pain. In due season, you will remember the pain. However, the reason for the remembrance of past pains is not for us to camp out in the remembrance and have a pity party. When we remember past pains, it will be during the times when He wants us to help others who are experiencing that same type of pain.

When the effects of pain are no longer felt, we also begin to have a *"heart of obedience."* John 14:15 reads, *"If ye love me, keep my commandments."* When our pain is wrapped in God's Glory, obedience will be our ultimate desire. We won't compromise with the devil. We will resist the devil and watch him flee from us. (James 4:7b)

Let me conclude this chapter by giving some effects of God's Glory. First, there will be a change in our relationship with God. It is impossible to experience the Glory of God and never have evidence of change. Change is inevitable. When Moses saw the revelation of God's glory, he quickly fell to his knees and worshipped. *Exodus 34:8 says "And Moses made haste, and bowed his head toward the earth, and worshipped."* At this point, Moses was *becoming intimate with God.* Moses was so stirred by God's Glory that he ran behind a rock, fell down, and worshipped. If you follow the scriptures, this was the first mention of Moses ever worshipping God in this manner. Before this incident, Moses had prayed to God. He had interceded for God's people. Moses had even sung to God, talked to God, and praised God. This is proof that we as Christian believers can talk, sing, pray, and even praise God, and yet not experience the real essence of God's Glory. Wow! That is serious! Can you imagine how many people go to church every time the door is opened, and never experience God's Glory! Some even work diligently in the church, but never experience God's Glory. Needless to say, that is sad.

So often it is pain that keeps us from experiencing God's Glory. When we release pain and get healed from our past, each level of healing will teach us how to worship God in *spirit* and in *truth*. Each level of healing will allow God to wrap our pain in His Glory. When God wraps our pain in His Glory, we immediately shift to another realm in the spiritual atmosphere.

Another effect of God's Glory is the "change in our countenance. "*Exodus 34:35 reads "And the children of Israel saw the face of Moses that the skin of Moses' face shone: and Moses put the veil upon his face again, until he went in to speak with him."* Our countenance is the outward expression of what is in our heart. When there is pain in our hearts, our outward expression will be that of sadness, despondency, and gloom. I remember people from various churches telling me how sad my countenance looked. I didn't realize I was looking sad, but my inward pain was reflecting on the outside. Moses' face reflected the Glory of God that was in his soul. Previous to this incident, Moses had been shut in with the Lord for 40 days and nights. There was no change in his countenance. Later, Moses came from God's holy presence to deal with idolatry of the golden calf. When the revelation of God's Glory was made real to him, it changed Moses' actual appearance! As stated earlier, when I was knotted in pain, my countenance looked painful and sad. But, when God wrapped my pain in His Glory, my countenance changed! The reflection of God's Glory was shining through me, and all over me! Not only did I recognize the change, but others did also!

Do you know that we can bask (relax) in God's presence all we want, but it is a different matter entirely for His Glory to be revealed in us. When God reveals His Glory within us, we no longer linger on *"what people say or think about us."* We care little about *'the doctrine of men.'* We no longer hold on to past pains and past offenses. Our countenance will give us away, when sin is there, just as it will, when the Glory of God is there. When the Glory of God is within us, our ultimate focus is on heavenly things, and not on the temporal things of the world.

The *"Glory of God"* is a wonderful, magnificent, breath-taking phenomenon that every Christian can experience. You will learn from reading this book that it is the Glory of God that can take away any of your pains. As you continue reading you will see how God literally took all of my pain, and wrapped it in His Glory! He can do the same thing for you!

Chapter 3

A Painful Mission:
Working As a Woman in Ministry

*A*fter many years of searching the scriptures, I learned that Jesus welcomed women into his private circle. Other than the twelve men who followed Jesus, there were also women who supported and followed Jesus. Women were not named in ancient texts unless they had social importance. Therefore, Jesus would often use the words *"and a certain woman."* Research lets us know however that there is a clear insinuation that wealthy women underwrote the Galilean mission. When Jesus welcomed women as his followers, this was highly unusual, because women didn't speak to men in public, nor did they travel the countryside with men. This concept of women reminds me of how I was reared. I grew up in a very traditional, *old-school* church in rural Mississippi. Now, in the small area where I lived, women did a lot of things to help build, restore, and oftentimes plant churches, but they were never given credit for doing so. They could never embrace the title of *Minister, Pastor, Bishop, Apostle,* or any other *so called masculine* title. To this day, my current titles of Apostle and Pastor is not recognized, acknowledged or welcomed by many people in my hometown (or the people who have moved away).

The fact that women could not hold the titles I mentioned earlier, or even operate in those offices was always strange to me. At the early age of 14 I had sensed a prompting from the Holy Spirit that a part of my mission while on planet earth was to be a preacher, teacher, and an evangelist. I did not know I would ever become a Pastor or an Apostle! The sadness and pain came to me when I was unable to share with others the words God had given to me. God spoke to me one day, and told me that *He wanted me to teach and preach the gospel of Jesus Christ.* Had I shared those words with others, I would have been re- buked and some of the church mothers probably would have begun to try and cast demons out of me.

During Jesus' resurrection, it was the woman who gave the message to the men. At first the apostles did not believe the messages from the women. And even today, some Disciples of Christ refuse to hear the gospel from the voice of the woman.[1] They fail to realize that women are the repairers of the breach in the Body of Christ.

"A breach is a broken section or gap in a wall, a fence or a hedge."[2] During the times of war, the breach was the place where the enemy came in to destroy camps. The breach was also where the sheep broke out of, and got lost. Repairing breaches is a never-ending task. Therefore, the women of God will con- tinue to be repairers of the breach, until the return of Jesus Christ. In spiritual matters, a breach in a defensive wall is even more serious, because it lets Satan in and encourages God's sheep to stray."[3]

In the course of studying about women in the church, I read a book by Lee Grady entitled *Ten Lies The Church Tells Women.* This book clearly proves that women can help to re- pair some of the breaches in the church. He identified many lies the church has told regarding women, and he explained to women why they should go forth in what God has called them to do. In the rest of this chapter, I will analyze some of

---

1   Future Church. (Cleveland, Ohio, 2001-2003) Info.futurechurch.org

2   David Loughran R., *Repairers Of The Breach,"* (Stewardson, Soctland:Stewarton Bible School, June 1999), 1.

3   Ibid.,

the lies Grady mentioned in his book and show you how God's Glory kept me through some of those same painful lies.

Lie number one stated, *"God's ultimate plan for women is that they serve their husbands."* [4] Grady clarified that God created Eve as a help meet or companion to man. She was man's completer, and not man's *maid* or *servant*. Women are actually co-laborers. Now, a lot of men in the church today would totally disagree with Lee. I whole-heartedly agree with him. The man should compensate the woman and the woman should compensate the man. They ultimately become one.

Often people go into marriages stating that they are going to give each other *50/50 percent*. God showed me how that concept is very wrong! Husbands and wives are to give each other *100/100 percent* of each other. Down through the years, I enjoyed fixing my husband's plate, and serving him, but it was not a mandate for me to do so. He in turn would often fix my plate and serve me. When the floors needed vacuuming or moping, he would do it, just as I would. Doing so did not take anything away from his masculinity. Actually, it enhanced his masculinity. My husband did not feel *it was not a man's job* to do the laundry, make the bed, or clean the bathroom. Many men do not feel this way. They want to be the only ones who are *served*. When a husband and wife support one another, the breach of a domestic slave or servant mentality is being repaired.

Lie number three declared that *"Women shouldn't work outside the home."* [5] For years, the church told women that they should be like the Proverbs 31 woman and take care of their husband and children. They were also told to work only in *lowly* or *humble* positions in the church. They could clean the church, cook for the church, and prepare the communion meal. I am assured that the church tends to misunderstand

---

4   Lee Grady, *Ten Lies The Church Tells Women."* p., 2. www.godswordtowomen.org/Lee-Grady.htm.
5   Ibid., 3.

the Proverbs 31 woman, when making those types of assumptions. The Proverbs 31 woman was *a real estate agent* and ran *a
textile business.*[6] What God wants from the woman is a balanced
life. He does not want her to put her career before Him, nor
her family. When women seek God's guidance, He will give
them a schedule that will permit them to have a balanced life.
Proverbs 3:6 states clearly, *"In all thy ways acknowledge Him, and
He shall direct thy paths." *[7]

I am a career woman. Had I not been, we might have had
many less meals, and we might have been homeless. God gave
me the grace to keep house, be a wife and mother, and yet
work in ministry. The hindering part was the fact that I could
not work the work that God had assigned me to do, because of
the tradition and religion of men. I am aware that some wom-
en get it twisted regarding ministry, but it was not so in my
case. I have heard some women say, *"Well, I have to do the work
of the Lord. I don't have time to fix dinner for my husband."* That's
not wisdom, and it will hinder and detour the call of God that
is on a woman's life. I made sure I took care of home first,
and then the ministry and others. Charity begins at home and
then spreads abroad.

Lie number four affirmed that *"Women must obediently
submit to their husbands in all situations." *[8] Grady gave this illustration in his book: *"A distraught Christian woman who was
regularly beaten by her husband finally gained the courage to seek
counsel from her pastor. After she told him about her husband's fits
of rage, the pastor responded, 'If your husband kills you, it will be to
the glory of God.'" *[9] That is what I call total insanity! Nothing
saddens me more than the images of women who have come
to church with blackened eyes, and walking with crutches and
canes, because of the physical abuse their *church going* (and in

6   Ibid., 3.
7   Holy Bible. King James Version.
8   Lee Grady, *Ten Lies The Church Tells Women."* p., 3. www.godswordtowomen.org/Lee-
Grady.htm.
9   Ibid. 3

some cases non-churched) husbands had given to them. And what is even more devastating is the response that the "narrow minded" mothers gave them: *"Baby just seek the Lord. Stay there with him. It is not the will of God to get a divorce."* Do yourself a favor before you read the next paragraph and just shout: *"The devil is a liar!"*

The church must get the false portrayal of marriage out of their souls. Marriages are seen as a hierarchy, with husbands on the throne and wives at the footstool. Ephesians 5:22 is always quoted, but often misunderstood. Many men fail to remember what Paul said in Ephesians 5:21. *"Submitting yourselves one to another in the fear of the Lord."* [10] That means that men are to submit to their wives, and the wives are to submit to their husbands. The church will be much stronger when pastors begin to tell the men that they are to be submissive also! [11] The demanding, dogmatic, power-driven man will get nothing but a "dead end," from a sure, steadfast, God-filled Proverbs 31 woman. When a woman knows who she is in Christ, she will not be controlled or abused by the man.

Lie number seven tells women *"They are not equipped to assume leadership roles."* [12] Too many people misinterpret I Timothy 2:12. *"But I suffer not a woman to teach, nor to usurp authority over the man, but to be in silence."* [13] There are many Biblical examples of women who had leadership roles. Deborah was a judge over Israel. Miriam and Huldah were leaders. Jesus' first gospel commission was to women. On the day of Pentecost both men and women were empowered to preach. Regardless of this seventh lie the church has told women, I am certain that God has equipped me to be a Leader, not only to women, but to men also. I have been in leadership roles since I was a teenager. At

---

10   Holy Bible King James Version.
11   Lee Grady, *Ten Lies The Church Tells Women."* p., 3. www.godswordtowomen.org/LeeGrady.htm
12   Lee Grady, *Ten Lies The Church Tells Women."* p., 5. www.godswordtowomen.org/LeeGrady.htm.
13   Holy Bible. King James Version.

the age of fourteen, adult men and women would come to me for Biblical and secular counseling. This stuff would blow my mind, but the Holy Spirit would give me what to tell these people. Yet today, many churches make a difference between carrying out a task and holding a position. They draw a fine line between allowing women to teach and preach versus letting them "hold the office" of teacher, preacher, pastor, bishop, or apostle. Repeatedly many churches deny women ministerial credentials and/or pastoral offices. For over half of my life, I was in traditional churches that would only give me a *missionary and/or an evangelist license*. Because I was connected with the organization, I had to submit to their rules. What often bewildered me was the fact that I did basically the same things I am doing now. I was preaching, teaching, and prophesying (along with other things that I do). In the previous organizations parishioners simply called what I was doing *good teaching and encouragement*.

In many cases, a woman could be responsible for planting a church, but not welcomed to become its official pastor. Women have also been moved to believe that God is willing to use them if, and only if men are not available. If that were the case, many churches and organizations would have never been founded. Consequently, after the dirty hard work had been done, a man became available to oversee the end result. This is totally unfair and ungodly.[14] I have the same attitude that Deborah had. If you are going to use my skills, you had better give the credit *to a woman*. Right is just right, regardless of your gender. Now, I hope the men of God continue reading the rest of this book. It gets better. I promise.

There have been instances where I could not stand in the pulpit and teach, because that area was called "holy sacred grounds," and only men were permitted to stand there. However, a small podium would be placed near the altar, and

---

14   Judy Brown, *"The Debate and Damage Continue."* (God's Word To Women), pp. 2-3. www.godswordtowomen.org/judy-brown.htm.

the same crowd would become receptive of the message God was speaking through me. Since there is a prophetic mantel over my life, I would often call people from the audience and minster to them. Or, I would walk over and minster to them (while I was teaching or preaching). However, I was instructed to never call up a man, because a woman should never give advice or tell a man what to do. I was also unable to lay hands on men. I was told that it was improper, and it was the role and duty of a man to lay hands on a man. As a result, I have been in services where there were wounded, hurting men, and I was able to discern their pain, but because of the tradition and religion of man, I could not pray with them. The sad part about this was that the men who were in the church were unable to discern the needs of the wounded, hurting men. Many men left the church with the same hurt and pain they brought with them. The church did not understand that hurting people, hurt people. In some cases after I finished ministering, the men would come to me and express their issues, and whisper to me, *"Sister, will you just pray for me. I wanted prayer during the services, but… You know how it is…"* This insanity has to stop! Men and women need to work together. Together we will stand, and divided we will fall! The wall of unity is torn, and women must help in repairing the breach in the Body of Christ!

Women have always taught men. Think about it. When little boys are growing up, they constantly remember those *golden nuggets* that a mother gave. They would often say, *"My mom told me that,"* or *"I need to ask my mom."* Even when men are in prison, they send messages back saying, *"Man, tell my momma I said hello,"* or *"Take care of my momma, now."* Women have always taught men! Where there's a successful man, it is certain that he can look back and give many testimonies of women who helped him to become successful!

Lie number ten indicated, *"Women who exhibit strong leadership qualities have a spirit of Jezebel."* [15] To associate godly women

---

15   Ibid., 7.

with Jezebel, a wicked Old Testament tyrant is unfair, insulting, and offensive. Men today are quick to label a woman as a Jezebel, if she is anointed, aggressive, and powerful. I have been told, *"You think you know it all,"* or *"Who gives you the authority to do that?"* When women walk in integrity and preach the Word of God, with the anointed power of the Holy Ghost, they deserve respect! Personally, I accept nothing less than respect. God has given me the authority and He has anointed and appointed me for a time such as this. I am on an assignment by the Most High God! I know who I am in Christ, and I know what I can do in Christ. I bear the Name of Jesus. I am washed in the blood of Jesus. I am in the family of God. In Jesus' Name I cast out demons. I resist the devil, and he flees from me. The devil is on the run. I am blessed coming in, and I am blessed going out. And whatever I put my hands to, I possess it. Having done all to stand, I stand. Healing is mine. Good health is mine. Prosperity is mine. The blessings of God are mine. I will not be ashamed of Jesus, nor His Word. I will bear the name that is above every name: The mighty, mighty name of Jesus! Hallelujah! Glory!

Yonggi Cho, pastor of the world's largest church was quoted saying, *"Don't be afraid to empower women."* [16] Cho went on to say, *"If you ever train the women, and delegate your ministry to them, they will become tremendous messengers for the Lord. In ministry they are equal with men. They are licensed. They are ordained. They become deaconess and elders."* [17] The majority of the leaders at Cho's church (Full Gospel Church in Seoul) are women. At one time, the 700,000-member congregation was divided into 50,000 cell groups that met in homes. About 47,000 cell leaders were women. There were 600 associate pastors, and 400 of them were women.[18]

---

16   *"Don't Be Afraid To Empower Women."*(Dawn Ministries), 1. http://www.godswordtowomen.org/Yonggi%20Cho.htm
17   Ibid., 1.
18   Ibid., 1.

Cho implemented the cell church theory in 1964 after he collapsed from exhaustion trying to minister to his (at that time) 3,000-member congregation. His male leaders did not totally agree when he told them to divide the congregation into cells that met in their homes. They said, *"Fine, but we are not trained to do that and we are not paid to do that. Why don't you have a long vacation?"* This was the Korean way of saying *"Why don't you resign from the church?"* [19] When Cho asked the women leaders to do it, they said, *"Teach us, pastor. We will do anything for you."* The church grew from 3,000 to 18,000 in the next five years." [20]

I recall a similar situation in my life. I was fortunate to have a pastor who allowed me to teach, preach, conduct revivals, and even administrate the church affairs in his absence. There was great church growth. However, after a while, some of the men, and even women began to cause a division. Some stated, *"She's doing everything." "I think you are giving her too much power, and authority."* Since there was so much contention, the pastor began to listen to them, and slowly released me of many of my duties, even before I really knew I was released. This caused great spiritual pain for me. I would come to church one day, and someone else was doing my previous job. Eventually, there was a sudden fall of membership. The anointing was dwindling, and things were not the same. If something works, why bother with it? I agree when Cho stated, *"It is the will of God to have a growing church."* [21] Whomever God uses to assist in church growth, the Body of Christ should receive that person, with a willing heart.

Finally, the question that has been asked for years must be answered. What is the woman's place? The woman's role is to assist in repairing all of the breaches in the Body of Christ. This chapter has only mentioned a few torn areas. There are numerous others. Until women begin to take a stand, they will

---

19   Ibid., 2.
20   Ibid. 2.
21   Ibid. 2

continue to reside on the back burners. They will continue to be labeled as a missionary, instead of a minister or preacher. Unfortunately, many women who are labeled as missionaries do not even have a mission. Women will continue to preach sermons that are called "good talks," or "good teachings." They will continue to preach from an area lower than the pulpit (or the holy place designated for men only). They will stand in front of a small podium, because the pulpit area is far too sacred for a woman to stand in. They will continue to clean, vacuum, mop, and dust the pulpit/platform area, but they will never teach, preach, prophecy, or minister from that area.

When the veil is removed from the eyes of men and women, the Body of Christ will become well rounded, productive, nourished, God-fearing Christians. Spiritual babies will not be born with defects, and others will not be aborted before their time of delivery. A spirit-filled, life flourishing anointing will be in the church for generations to come. Finally, Judy L. Brown stated, "*Those who favor women ministers must not only act on their convictions; they must also challenge and correct those who discriminate against women. Of course, this must be done thoughtfully and wisely; but, if it is not done at all, then the wrongdoing will continue.*" [22] The women of God must rise up and take their place in the Kingdom of God. If women adhere to Proverbs 3:5-6, they will be in their rightful places. Proverbs 3:5-6 says " *5 Trust in the Lord with all thine heart; and lean not unto thine own understanding. 6 In all thy ways acknowledge him, and he shall direct thy paths.*"

---

22   Judy L. Brown, *"The Debate and Damage Continue."* (God's Word To Women), p. 7. www.godswordtowomen.org/judy-brown.htm.

Chapter 4

Inheriting A Church Full Of Hurting People: Operating Under The Surgical Anointing

*G*od has placed a *surgical anointing* within me to help those who have had inner damages so deep, that it almost took the very life from them. Most people have experienced physical, financial, and social problems, but the worst afflictions to a person are the afflictions from a spiritual injury. It supersedes any other type of wound. It offends and distresses so deeply that an individual feels all hope is gone. Often, people who have been wounded spiritually tend to act and function like a nervous wreck. Their emotions and spirits are literally crippled. Since we as humans exist in three parts (body, soul, and spirit), the spirit is what relates to the soul, which in turn relates to the body. When the spirit is wounded, the soul and body feels the damages, and immediately needs spiritual surgery, in order to have a thorough healing. I am confident that after reading this chapter, and going through the process of spiritual healing, your life will never be the same. Your body, soul, and spirit will soar into new dimensions that you would have never imagined. You must remind yourself over and over again that you were fearfully and wonderfully made, and that life is worth the living.

Over nine years ago, my husband and I inherited a church full of hurting people, and this is when I began to operate under what God voiced to me as a "surgical anointing." Upon receiving these people in our church, we learned quickly that they were "emotionally crippled," because of years of spiritual wounds.

We had been attending a ministry that was filled with people who were being molested and rapped spiritually, and some even literally, by the pastor. I used the word "molested," because to them, the pastor was their "spiritual father." The people were brainwashed into feeling that everything they were doing, was "in the Name of Jesus." The pastor robbed these people of their dignity, self-worth, monies, spouses, and whatever the people allowed him to take. Many of the members of the church were spiritually, emotionally, mentally, and almost physically dead. Even to this day, some of them have not recovered from the devastation and pain.

Since this chapter's focus is about spiritual healing, I believe it is necessary to give a definition of a distressed, injured, or wounded spirit. A distressed, injured, or wounded spirit is known as a *broken spirit* or *crushed spirit*. The Bible says, *"A man's spirit sustains him in sickness, but a crushed spirit who can bear?"* (Proverbs 18:14) It also states *"A cheerful heart is good medicine, but a crushed spirit dries up the bones."* (Proverbs 17:22)

The spirit part of a person is *the engine* to his/her life. It is *the mere essence of life.* No matter how beautiful and expensive the body may look, life is broken without its spiritual performance. In fact, the breakdown of the spirit eventually brings sickness to the body. It dries up the bones. I learned this early on as a young pastor that many of the people who were wounded spiritually had all kinds of physical ailments. They had high blood pressure, diabetes, arthritis, nervous disorders, and other sicknesses.

A wounded spirit is not just among people who are of a lower economic status, either. Actually, those with wealth are

34

sometimes wounded the most. Some of the people in the aforementioned church had monies. They had good jobs. They
were educators. A wounded spirit affects all economic groups.
Luke 12:15 says, *"Watch out! Be on your guard against all kinds
of greed; a man's life does not consist in the abundance of his posses-
sions."* Money can buy a lot of things, but it cannot buy total
happiness. Hence, the church mentioned earlier in this chapter was filled with unhappy, unfortunate, displeased people.
And you may ask, *"Well, why didn't they leave that church?"* It was
because pain became a stronghold on them, and they did not
recognize the source of their spiritual distress and wounds.

When trying to understand the source of the people's
wounds, I began to do some research. I read some powerful
articles from the *Jesus Work Ministry,* an online resource that
dealt with Spiritual Warfare. From those articles, I learned that
the sources of spiritual wounds are called *avenues.* Avenues are
where spiritual wounds come from. They are doorways (Jesus
Work Ministry). Satan gains legal entry in his mission to *"steal,
kill, and destroy,"* through the doorways. When ministering to
the wounded souls I inherited, I noticed four doorways that
Satan gained entrance. Those doorways were *deception, ignorance, sin, and storms of life.* His entry through any of these
doorways can bring *"spiritual injuries and wounds,"* that will re-
quire a *"spiritual healing."* (Jesus Work Ministry)

Deception is done by way of trickery, dishonesty, fraud, and
cheating. There have been many articles published regarding
pastors who failed, because of deception. They allowed the
glamour, fame, and beauties of life to become a distraction.
These distractions wounded a lot of good-hearted people.
Many people who came to our ministry had seen firsthand
how their previous pastor had taken money and misused it.
They saw personally what pastoral deception could do to a
congregation. Former members testified how thousands of
dollars would come through the church weekly, but there
was always a *so-called lack.* There was lack with the bills in the

church being paid; employees hardly ever received their pay-checks from the school the church owned, and the list goes on and on. This misuse of funds led to a lot of spiritual wounds. Since false teachings also fall under the doorway of decep-tion, many of the congregants were falsely told that God was in everything they were doing and that they should continue to give money to the *"work of the Lord."* The main work (or so called work) was that of the pastor's pocket and bank account. The congregants were constantly told that it was their fault that the bills were not paid. They were told that it was their fault that the employees were not paid. This incurred deep spiritual injuries and wounds, because the people knew they had given all they had, to no avail.

Because of deception regarding money, once these people joined our ministry, it took over two years of constant teach-ing, encouragement, and spiritual impartation to get the peo-ple back into *the mindset* that *giving* was the will of God. They were hesitant because the injuries and wounds of deception kept opening up on the inside of them, and the memory was something they did not want to relive through another pas-tor. The journey was long, but it was worth the travel. Now, we have people in our church who have become "pay masters." Pay Masters are people who go far beyond tithes and regular offerings. They are the people who help sustain the ministry. They are the people who God takes to higher dimensions eco-nomically, because of their giving. They trust God totally in their giving, because they are constantly receiving and reap-ing from the Lord's harvest of blessings.

Ignorance is another dangerous thing that can cause spiri-tual injuries and wounds. When someone is *deceived, ignorance* is manifested and magnified (Jesus Work Ministry). When there is a lack of knowledge, people are vulnerable to fall victim of Satan's deception and false doctrines. It is vital that intense reading and studying of God's Word is done often. Even though the Word was preached and taught in this aforementioned church, the people remained ignorant. They only ate the part of the Word that they wanted to eat, or that they were told to eat. Consequently, the lack of knowledge permitted blindfolds to be over their eyes regarding the deceit they were underneath. Ignorance told them that everything that was happening was directly in the plan and will of God. When the blindfolds were finally removed, many had anger and bitterness that enveloped them to the point of almost not living for God and believing in the Bible, entirely. Some of them even had desires to literally kill the pastor! I am reminded of one late night counseling session where my husband and I had to really intercede for a gentleman. He was headed to the previous pastor's house, to kill him. Again, it took over two years or more to help the people receive and accept knowledge concerning the things of God. Midnight counseling and warfare prayers went forth weekly, to help with deliverance and inner healing. Many shut-ins (all-night prayer and consecration services) took place. Many tears were shed. But joy came in the morning!

Sin accompanies ignorance and deceit. Whether committed knowingly or out of ignorance, sin has the same consequences (Jesus Work Ministry). The worst of sins that can bring a severe wounded spirit include involvement in *occult practices*, and *sexual sins*. A plethora of occult practices and sexual sins took place in the church that was previously mentioned in this chapter. The word "occult" refers to what is hidden, concealed, or secret. There were so many secrets and hidden things in that church until it will blow the average churchgoer's mind. There was a spirit of unfathomable control and micro-management over the congregants. If the pastor did not like a particular person, soon everyone knew it, and the rest of the congregation did not like the person either. That's a mess! The church would treat the person (or should I say victim) like those who had leprosy were treated in Biblical times. Any degree of occult involvement can produce problems of oppression, depression, despair, hopelessness, and many physical problems. These problems sometimes bring death and even self-destruction. Demonic influences can produce obsessions, phobias, bizarre behaviors, violence, homicide and sexual perversion in its victims.

There were many days and nights during the spiritual surgery and recovery process where I had to literally pull off different phobias and bizarre behaviors that plagued the congregants. People were afraid to go outside their homes alone. Many were afraid to do anything in the church, such as teaching, singing, reading a scripture, or collecting the offering. They would say, *"Pastor, I used to do this, but I forgot how."* The minds and spirits of these people were so damaged until God had to work a miracle in their lives, to bring healing and deliverance.

Also, almost every woman who came to our ministry had the same exact story, with the same *"exact play"* that the pastor made on them. It was like a cancer! It was like a deadly virus! Marriages were torn apart, and mothers and daughters are fighting among themselves, to this day, because of the sexual sins that were committed by the previous pastor. In all of this disaster, many souls were dying, and eventually some of them came to the place where they never wanted to walk into another church door again.

Sadly, it was only a few years later that the pastor went to a nearby city and started another church. My heart was saddened, because of the new victims he was inflicting. Recently, he has come back to the city where our ministry is, and tried to lure some of the members from our church to come and join him in his new ministry. This madness in the Body of Christ has got to stop! God is not pleased with this type of behavior! Sin stinks in the nostrils of God.

Finally, Storms of Life is simply those unpleasant experiences that come upon each of us, because of no fault of our own. These include experiences of living under constant negative and critical words, experiences of betrayal *(by a loved one, trusted person, or leader*), death of a loved one, severe physical or emotional abuse experiences, or living under rejection (Jesus Work Ministry).

When storms of life occur, there are both mental and emotional effects. Examples of mental effects include recurring bad dreams, memories of past hurts, focusing on faults, and difficulty in forgiving. When this happens, the victims actually re-live the damaging experiences. A lot of the members of the aforementioned church went through years of bad dreams and bad memory recalls. The surgical anointing allowed me to re-direct their thinking. I had to daily walk them through the Word, and I had to constantly remind them to think on things that were pure, pleasant, honest, and of a good report.

Emotional effects that many of the people experienced included being withdrawn (introversion) or too outgoing (extroversion). With both emotional effects, the people tended to be fearful, suspicious, and often had overwhelming feelings of distress. When this happened, their will was affected. Sometimes when I thought we had taken one step of victory forward, suddenly, the emotional effects of fear took some of the people by the throat, nearly strangling the life out of them. At that point they sometimes took five steps backwards. It was an ongoing warfare.

Some of the people became workaholics, reckless, stubborn, domineering, weak-willed, self-centered, and insensitive to correction. As I recall the introvert members, they were extremely withdrawn from people. One lady in particular would become very anxious and nervous around two or more people. She would just *'shut-down,'* and not talk, or she would begin to tremble and cry. Actually, she wouldn't even go to the grocery store alone, in fear of people watching her. A feeling of unmanageable shame and guilt would try to smother her. Constant prayer and warfare pulled her through this.

During all of those episodes with the congregants, God revealed to me that He was placing within me, *"a surgical anointing."* He often showed me medical instruments in the spirit as I counseled and ministered to people. These instruments were used spiritually to perform what God gave me as, *"spiritual surgery."* Each individual became a spiritual patient. In seeing medical instruments in the spirit, God had caused me to use some of the actual methods of performing a physical surgery, in working with those who had been "wounded and injured spiritually." He showed me how to prepare someone for spiritual surgery, what to except during pre-op, and He then walked me through things I must do during surgery. Afterwards, God instructed me on what to do with patients (the members) during recovery. He let me know that physical recovery was an on-going process. Hence, *'spiritual healing'* is an ongoing process also.

With physical surgery, most people don't have surgery without the knowledge of being diagnosed with something. The medical doctor tells us what the *"diagnosis"* is. In dealing with the spiritually wounded, I had to allow the Holy Spirit to instruct me as to what the *"condition"* or diagnosis was. After I realized what the condition was, I had to let the *"patient"* (the member) know what his/her condition was. If we don't know what areas we need "healing in," or what we need healing from, we will walk around with the disease, and the pain will continue. If the pain continues, it will begin to bring damage to other areas of our lives, just as cancer or any other physical disease would.

For example, God would instruct me in telling the members what type of fear they had. For others who had the spirit of lust, God allowed me to walk them back through their childhood genesis of where lust began. Then, He would instruct me on how to process them through their past experience, and help them to make a new experience take place in their minds. Afterwards God let me walk them into a new present state of mind, where deliverance would often take place.

After advising the patient of surgery, the medical doctor then walks the patient through the process of what he/she will be doing during surgery. I told the people of whom I ministered to that *"inner healing"* is a very serious thing, and I walked them through the many things I would be doing during the surgical process. For example, I let them know that God would literally allow me to pierce into their souls (minds) to bring up experiences from their past. When the past was revealed, it was done by way of dreams, or I could have been talking about an event that triggered the person's memory. While talking, sometimes the person would begin to say, *"I am remembering what happened to me in the office of the church."* Eventually, tears would begin to fall from their faces. At this point the Holy Spirit would give me the right tools (words) to say, to walk the person back through the experience, but leaving the moment in their minds, in a different way. If in the actual experience the person left the incident feeling extreme shame and pain, guilt, and like the whole thing was his/her fault, I would show the person how to relive it, but leave the incident feeling, thinking, and talking a positive way. Afterwards, this part of the surgery would have ended. The healing journey did not end there.

Nevertheless, I had to constantly remind the people that in spiritual healing, the *"ultimate manifestation"* (the date of surgery or completion of the surgery) could take place at any time. Unlike the *"physical surgery,"* the *spiritual surgery* is an ongoing process, until different levels or dimensions of healing takes place. With this inner-healing, I let the person know I would be asking him/her pronging questions that would wake up the sub-conscience, in areas of their spirits that would have been dormant. Or, in some cases those areas would have never been touched. Medical doctors do the same thing, and afterwards, the medical doctor sets a date for surgery. Again, with spiritual healing, we have to let people know that the "ultimate manifestation" (the date or the completion of the surgery) could take place at any time, and anywhere. Unlike the "medical surgery," the spiritual surgery is an on-going process.

Just before medical surgery, we normally do a pre-op. This is where vital signs are taken, and a medical history is done, and different waivers are signed. As a Spiritual Surgeon, before digging deep into the spirit of a person, a *pre-op* has to be completed. This is where some questions will be asked about the person's past. Answers to these questions allow the Spiritual Surgeon to hear from God as to which method should be used in performing the surgery. One must always remember that each case is different. The method used for one person might not work for another person. *"He that has an ear, let him hear what the Spirit is saying unto the church."* This pre-op method of asking questions will also prepare the Spiritual Surgeon as to what he/she will be faced with during surgery. The more severe the spiritual damage, the more intense the surgery will be.

Finally, when patients have a medical surgery, they are told not to eat after a certain time. As a Spiritual Surgeon, I had to encourage the people to begin times of fasting. The time of fasting is essential, because it allows the person to operate in the spirit, and not the flesh. Fleshy thoughts will cause fleshy emotions and wills, and divert what God wants to do spiritually. Without fasting, the spiritual surgery will be harmful to an individual. Incidents could come to mind from the past, and it might make a person sicker than he/she was before the spiritual surgery.

With physical surgery, patients are connected to an Intravenous Machine (IV), and eventually sedated. The IV ensures that the right amount of fluids continue to flow through the body, in order to sustain life. Spiritually, this was a time when I had to encourage the people I was working with to connect as often as possible to the Holy Spirit. That meant staying in God's presence by spending much time in prayer, meditation, reading and studying God's Word, worshipping and praising God, attending church regularly, and spiritual and sometimes professional counseling. In doing so, the Holy Spirit was going to sedate them from the *"wounds and injuries of their past."* After being sedated, the medical Surgeon is able to work on the individual. I found that after people were *"sedated in the presence of God,"* at any time, I was able to do some cutting. When we are in God's presence, we don't *"feel the pain"* from the cutting. That is part of what is meant by *"God wrapping your pain in His Glory."* God's Glory gives numbness to the pain and allows the Holy Spirit to operate and function effectively.

Sometimes during medical surgery, the anesthesia wears off before the surgery is complete. At this point, the medical doctor has to add more sedating medication through the IV. I noticed that when the *"spiritual anesthesia"* wore off, I was not able to cut, without causing even more pain. The Spiritual Anesthetic wore off when the patients came *"out of the presence of God."* During spiritual surgery, we have to constantly remind our patients the importance of staying in the presence of God! Again, this is done by a consistent time of meditation, prayer, reading and studying God's Word, worshipping and praising God, attending church services, and spiritual counseling (and oftentimes professional counseling).

Sometimes after a physical surgery, patients are taken to the Intensive Care Unit (ICU). While in ICU, the patient is monitored *"around the clock."* I remember the many days and nights after spiritual surgery that I had to be on the phone, or right there in the presence of some people, because that short period after spiritual surgery was critical. During this time, I would check their *spiritual vital signs* often. This was done by asking questions about their emotions and state of being. As always, the Holy Spirit would give me directions on what to say to them. Too often have people been opened up with reminders from their past, but the person who opened them left them open and bleeding, without any after treatment or care.

Some have literally died spiritually, from being left open to the spirit of the air (Satan and his imps). We as believers must never forget that we are in a spiritual warfare. Satan is the spirit of the air, and he is roaming to and fro, seeking whom he may devour.

After a period of time in ICU (with a physical surgery), the patient is then sent to a regular floor, and eventually he/she goes home. With severe surgeries *(Actually, all of the people God used me to do spiritual surgery with, were severe.)*, going home required therapy. With Spiritual Healing, therapy was very vital. I found that therapy meant moving and doing, so you can get better. Therefore, the method God gave me deviated from what traditional and religious people would normally believe, or think spiritual therapy should be. When I say *"moving and doing,"* I mean actually working in ministry. I did not have a set time for each member, as to when he/she would start moving and working in ministry, because each person was different. And each situation was different. If it was left up to many of the members, they wouldn't have been working in ministry at all, even to this day! In their past ministry experiences, they were always told that they should not work in ministry, if they had *"issues."* Well, if that was the case, no one would be working in ministry. We all have issues!

In saying that, once the members had gone through a *"radical spiritual surgery,"* I began *"radical spiritual therapy."* The Radical Therapy God gave me meant *"activating the gifts"* within people that had been dormant because of being *"spiritually wounded."* Now, as with physical therapy, many of the people that God used me to perform Spiritual Surgery on did not like spiritual therapy. They wanted to *'sit and do nothing in ministry until they felt they were healed.'* They were always taught that *"Hurting people, hurt people."* I had to remind them that what they were taught was true. However, they also had to learn that *"Healed people, heal people."* After a certain period of time, God instructed me to not allow them to sit and just do nothing in the church. For many years, their gifts had already been dormant, and that is what led to their past spiritual illness.

Eventually, during spiritual therapy, most of the *'spiritual patients (members)''* realized that the radical spiritual therapy was the element that allowed them to come alive again. Many of them actually became anointed intercessors, ministers, elders, musicians, armor bearers, and pastors. Not only that, many of them began to give Word of Knowledge and prophetic utterances to the Body of Christ. Their mindsets literally changed for the better. They were able to give life to others. They were able to identify all of the doorways that the devil uses to damage believers.

Those who looked on from the outside expected the people who had such drastic spiritual wounds and injuries to yet be walking around with bandages, and canes. They expected them to lose their minds and never function in ministry again. Well, I must say this with holy boldness: *The devil is a liar*! Instead, they were leaping and praising God for what He had done in their lives! I must note, however, that recovery is an on-going process. Sometimes, when there are triggers (just like when bad weather triggers and causes pain, after physical surgery), God has to give reminders and the medicines of His Word to put them back on track, and remove the pain.

From hearing God, I have seen people come from little self-esteem, shyness, shame, guilt, frustration, rejection, pride, anger, bitterness, suspense, nervousness, and a whole lot of other things, to whole complete individuals. For those whom God has entrusted with me, the change took a while to manifest, but it was well worth it. Many of the people have grown to a place in God that was unimaginable to them, as well as others, before their Spiritual Surgery. When God gave me this method, onlookers did not believe I was hearing from God. They would make comments like: *"Oh God, do you know what they did? They are not ready for ministry. Lord, you are a young pastor. You don't know any better. Poor thing, you don't know what you are doing."*

My comfort was this: God told me that *"He would move quickly on the people's behalf."* He said to me, *"The wounds were great, and they could cause permanent damage. Some will receive, but others won't. Don't worry. Work with those who want to be helped."* As I worked with various individuals, I constantly reminded them that God was going to move quickly. I would always tell them these three words: *"God got it!"* And it took the faith of both the Spiritual Surgeon and the Spiritual Patient to know that God *"really had it."* Those three words, *"God got it,"* brought each of us through the tough, tear-shedding, spiritual wounds and injuries in our lives. I say *"ours,"* because all of us had been wounded and injured from the previous ministry. When our sisters and brothers hurt, each of us should hurt with them.

"Those who are willing and obedient will eat the good of the land." God will do whatever we allow Him to do. When we draw close to God, and connect with the Holy Spirit, the results of God's blessings are beyond our imagination. When we continue to obey God, our healing progresses and a healthy spirit sets in. As God works through us, we are able to effectively impact the world, for Jesus Christ.

Chapter 5

The Devil Tried To Kill My Baby: My Encounter With Infidelity

This chapter is actually the main chapter that prompted me to write the story of my life. This chapter gave me a clearer revelation of what my *'purpose is'* while I am on planet earth. When God delivers and restores us, it is not totally for us. It is for our good, but ultimately, it is for God's Glory! He gets the Glory when we tell others about our story, so they too can get deliverance.

As I matured in God, I truly understood John 10:10. *"The thief cometh not, but for to steal, and to kill, and to destroy: I am come that they might have life, and that they might have it more abundantly."* You see, God has impregnated everyone with a promise. I knew at this point in my life that the devil was trying to kill my *baby.* When saying "baby," I mean the "promise or promises" He had given to me regarding my destiny. The devil wanted to nullify everything that God said He was going to fulfill in my life. This chapter is causing me to be very transparent, and I am choosing to do this because the Holy Spirit has prompted me to do so. I am certain that there are many women in the church who have gone through similar traumatic experiences, and don't know what to do, or who to go to for help. Sadly, there are many who are yet going through similar situations. Therefore, see this chapter as a time for *change, restoration, spiritual maturity*, and *a chance to move into a new dimension in God,* like never before.

My husband and I have been married for over 28 years, and many people saw our marriage and our family as the *perfect American family:* Mom, Dad, a boy, a girl, and a dog. What could be better? Like other married couples, we have had our share of life's ups and downs. There have been times when I would feel as though things were not right, but I ignored them, or denied the signals. I did not know why my husband was rarely compassionate or romantic. He was in the military, and he would blame his lack of compassion and romance on his busy schedule, or the extreme fatigue that his job imposed upon him. Sometimes he would blame his upbringing, of not having a 'male role model' to look up to.

Our marriage was a constant roller-coaster. And, it was only after serious disagreements that he would cater to me and my physical, mental, and emotional needs. However, those feelings would never last for more than three weeks or so. Afterwards, it was back to the same longing desires of my being suitably loved and romanced by my husband. I wanted him to say, *"sweet nothings to me,"* and just *"embrace me,"* for no reason at all. Disappointedly, my husband would always be concerned for the needs of others, and he would say wonderful things to them, but not to me. If it weren't for the strength I had within, and if God had not wrapped my pain in his Glory, my self-esteem would have been crushed and slaughtered. All the while, everyone who knew us envied our relationship. Through all of this, I never scandalized his name or put him down in front of others. Actually, I always addressed him to the public as *my lover, my companion, and my king.* I was trying to speak things into existence. I was standing on the Word of God, which He spoke in the scriptures to His people.

As for our children, I was basically Mom and Dad. I went to almost every school event, catered to their needs, and taught them how to reverence God. My husband was there, but *'not there.'* As with me, the children never received a lot of compassion, hugs or kisses from their dad. My son did not have the joy of playing football or any sports with his dad. However, I must give my husband some credit. He did take our son to Boy Scout and soccer events. But that was the extent of the father and son bonding. It was always constant military demands and yelling. Again, many people on the outside saw none of this. All of the children envied my daughter and son, because they felt that my children had the most wonderful Dad in the world. They felt that our children lived the lifestyle of the *"rich and famous."* Just as with me, my children accepted this life, and the three of us grew closer and closer to each other. That's probably why many people don't understand our closeness. The three of us were basically all we had: each other.

What the outside world saw were the provisions we had. My husband was and still is an excellent provider. Neither I, nor my children ever wanted for hardly any material things. If I dreamed it, my husband would do whatever it took to materialize it. I have had some of the best cars, from Infinities to Mercedes. We have had beautiful homes, and our current home is gorgeous. My children and I could shop basically anywhere we wanted to shop. The fineries of life were given to us. Hence, to the outside world, we appeared to be *the perfect family.*

The moment that brought all of us to a crossroad of *decisions, emotions, devastation, and trauma* was one cold Christmas vacation. That holiday was far from a white Christmas. It ended up being a dark, black, morbid, sad Christmas. The truth that was kept a secret for many years was brought to light during this supposedly joyous, festive, holiday occasion.

I did not receive this gruesome, horrible, shocking truth until after we had all made it back home to Florida. When we made it back to Florida, I found out why things had not been so great in our marriage. It was that cold winter when I found out that my husband had not been faithful (for over 20 years) to his marriage vows. When I found out, I felt like my whole world had stopped. Again, my body became very stiff and numb. All life seemed to have drained from me. I felt all sorts of emotions: anger, deep sorrow, regret, and disappointment.

When infidelity happens, there is a flood of emotions that encompasses a person, and these emotions feel destructive, like a hurricane. When something this drastic happens, it is normal to spill those emotions onto your family and friends, and this is what I did. However, when I spilled them, I was bashed, harshly spoken to, and was told, *"I should have never disrobed a King."* Those words of disrobing a king was uttered by my former pastor.

When my pastor spoke those words to me, my world stopped again. I was told that I should have never told anyone before coming to him first. Now, in my mind, I was thinking: *"I am a woman. He is a man."* A man had just hurt me badly. Why would I go to another man for help? At that moment, I was distraught. Yet again, another man was hurting me, and he made it seem as though it was all my fault. I was feeling lost, confused, and overwhelmed, and I did not know what to do. My body stiffened, and the ribbon of abuse began to grow even longer.

Allow me to go back a few weeks earlier, before this incident (and before this cold Christmas), so I can explain the constant stiffness I was feeling. A few weeks prior, I had been given a doctor's report that had changed my world, even to this day. For about four years, I had been having symptoms of extreme fatigue, lack of coordination, weakness, and numbness in my legs, hands and arms. There were other symptoms also. The doctor had informed me that I had the incurable disease of Multiple Sclerosis (MS). Multiple Sclerosis or MS is a disease that affects the brain and spinal cord, resulting in loss of muscle control, vision, balance, and sensation (such as numbness). When stress is increased, a person is likely to have a relapse. Severe pain accompanies an MS relapse. The body sometimes stiffens.

Knowing what stress could do to my body, I had to think quickly, on what path I would take. Almost instantly, my husband started to receive what was called *'counseling,'* from our pastor. I was receiving basically nothing, for almost a month. My husband and I decided it was best for him to leave the house for a while, so the both of us could think. Since I am bi-vocational, I had to continue being a pastor, a professor at the local community college, mother, friend, aunt, counselor, etc. I was beyond exhaustion. After about a month, the pastor advised me to read one of Joyce Meyer's book entitled: *The Root of Rejection.* I was like, *"Huh?"* Out of *obedience, I read the book.* The church always taught us to obey the pastor, because they were the watchmen of our souls. So, I read the book. But reading the book alone was a bit much. I needed a human there who would help me pull things together on the inside of me. Life had given me a rather bitter pill to swallow, and I needed help! I needed a Spiritual Surgeon!

Eventually, I agreed to let him come back home. I must admit, I did not like my husband at all. I don't believe I hated him, because I was always taught to never hate anyone. But, I did know I was no longer *in love* with him. I would preach often on loving your enemies and praying for those who despitefully used you, so there I was, trying to *"walk out, or live by those words."* That was a hard task. Besides, I had been faithful to one man, for almost half of my life. I felt betrayed. I felt lost.

My husband eventually began to express some of his feelings to me. He said he felt shame and embarrassment, and didn't want anyone to know about our personal business. You see, the word got out about his infidelity. That happens quickly in small towns. However, let me share with you one way the news about the infidelity came about.

Our church decided to have our annual *"Highly Favored Women's Conference."* Wow, for a while afterwards, I had to

wonder if we were *highly favored*. We were having the conference because the same pastor had invited a speaker to his
church during one of his church conferences, which actually
transformed many lives, spiritually. Some of our church members, along with my husband had attended. I had something
else to do, so I could not attend. I can't remember right now,
what it was I had to do. However, everyone came back talking
of how great of a speaker/preacher the lady who spoke, was,
and that I should invite her to our church. Well, I didn't feel
it, after viewing her video, and decided not to mention her
name again, unless my husband or the members mentioned
her. Well, they did, and before long I contacted her, and our
church continued the plans for our *"Highly Favored Women's
Conference."*

We had several speakers, but one of the speakers was Pastor
Paula Edwards, who wrote the book entitled: *A Resurrected Hoe:
From Hoe To Hero.* It's a must read, and I highly encouraged
everyone to read it. The conference was one-of-a-kind. But
the last day topped any conference I had ever attended in my
life! In the final service, one of the women from our church
asked if she could testify. I concurred, and she got up and said,
*"Pastor, I know this woman is from God. I was blessed and delivered
from the Word she gave, and from her testimony. And I just want to
say, I used to be a hoe. Actually, I was a midnight hoe. But today, I
thank God that He has delivered me from being a hoe. And I decree
and declare that none of my children nor grandchildren will ever be a
hoe....!"* Well, that came as a mouth-opening and jaw-dropping
surprise! But what happened afterwards, floored everyone. I
simply said, with a laugh, *"My God, are there any more testimonies?
Are there any more former hoes who want to testify?"* Well, I was just
asking, so we could go on to the next aspect of our service, and
certainly did not expect a response. I just wanted to shift the
shock that was in the atmosphere (so I thought), until nearly
15 more people got up and began to testify. I had never seen
such. And, I have never seen anything like it since then either.

After each person finished testifying, I simply asked the same question I had asked earlier: *"My God, are there any more testimonies. Are there any more former hoes who want to testify?"* People testified of being previous Sanctified Hoes, Universal Hoes, and a Sophisticated Hoe. Those names were just some of the names given by the people making the testimonies. Despite what was said afterwards about the church service, (in which I will mention later) I am confident that the service was orchestrated by God, and not me.

Everything was moving right along, until my husband stood up and testified. He said, *"Well, I was a Mississippi Hoe, and had been cheating on my wife for many years. But, today, I am glad that God has delivered me!"* The church was in a stupor. Now, I was in shock also. But, being the senior pastor of the church, I had to control my countenance, and just shout for the victory, like everyone else. After thinking back on the response I made afterwards, I now know I should not have responded in that manner. However, after my husband's comments, I was beginning to feel numb and stiffened again, and I just reacted spontaneously, by saying, *"Well, praise God for deliverance, because if that Mississippi hoe had not confessed and come forth during this anointed service, I was going to divorce him."* The conference ended in what we all thought was a *'bang!'*

After service, we all went to dinner at a local restaurant, but the table felt weird, especially from my husband's side. I couldn't quite figure out what was wrong, because everyone else at the table was yet talking about how free they felt, and how happy they were for their deliverance and the feeling of freedom they felt on the inside. Let me back track for a minute. Before we walked into the restaurant, I had spoken with our former pastor on the phone, and told him everything that had happened. I thought he was happy for everyone. I did discern however, that he was in disbelief, because he had never heard of that type of confessing. Neither had any of us heard of it! It wasn't until we made it home, that *'all hell broke loose again.'* My husband had talked to the pastor, and had given him a different version of what took place in that service.

Upon finally settling down for the evening, my husband said, *"Why did you make that statement? You embarrassed me! Why did you say you were going to divorce me?"* My response was, *"Well, it was the truth. I had made up my mind to divorce you a long time ago. But I want to be with you. I want us to make this thing work."* He then stated, *"That wasn't deliverance. You forced me to do that! You forced all those people to do that!"* Once again, my world stopped, and I was numb and stiffened. By then, MS was kicking in overdrive. I responded, *"I did not force anyone to do anything!"* We began to go back and forth: *"You coerced those people into saying all that stuff! You made them come up in front of the church and say all of that stuff!"* Evidently he had told the pastor the same thing, because when I spoke with the pastor again, I was reprimanded badly. He even said, *"Girl, that wasn't God. God doesn't do that kind of stuff. That was a mess. Now what? Now what are you going to do, that everyone knows your business? I don't know how to help you out of this mess!"*

That was the day I made up in my mind that he did not have to worry about helping me ever again. The relationship between me and that pastor had to end. It did not end in a pleasant way, but eventually it did. Regretfully, it was a very bitter ending. The memory of the bitter ending made me sad, for a very long time.

Much happened in those years afterwards, but the pages of a book cannot hold all of it. Perhaps some of the other people involved with that cold winter nightmare will write their books and give their side of the story. I was commissioned to only tell my life's story.

Chapter 6

BEING A RECIPIENT OF
THE SURGICAL ANOINTING

*A*s stated in Chapter 5, many eventful things took place in my life, but after some years, my husband had to leave to go and defend our country overseas. After my husband left the country, the loneliness I felt cannot be described in words. And even though I have a Master's degree in the English language, my vocabulary is too limited to express the pain and sorrow I felt within. I went into a slight depression, but not enough where I could not function. I yet preached, counseled people (even couples), prophesied, held down a church, and managed a functional school. I also continued working at the local community college as a professor. I am sure there were many days that I appeared sad and distraught to my colleagues, but I could not express what I was feeling. Besides, who would a pastor tell this type of drama to? Several of my colleagues knew of my health issues, so they probably assumed I was always feeling sick. Well, they were right about not feeling well. I did always feel sick: physically, emotionally, socially, intellectually, and at times, spiritually.

During this time of my life, as I ministered, people were healed and delivered, but I was dying on the inside. My health was weakening daily. During the day, I was a superhero. But at night, Wonder Woman took off her cape and she wrapped her pain in God's Glory, so she could survive (live). At night I would travail and cry out to God. Sometimes I would read God's Word. At other times, I would just be silent, and listen to God to see what He was saying to me.

It wasn't until about two months later that I decided to seek some professional counseling. I understood that I did not need to fall deep into depression, and I also understood that it was dangerous to bleed all of my silent emotions onto our congregation. I randomly chose a counselor from my insurance list under the *"Christian Counseling,"* heading. Being very apprehensive, I made the call, and explained my life's story. Immediately, I was given an appointment. Two days later, I was driving to the counselor's office. After arriving in the parking lot, I almost changed my mind, but I finally made it to the door. The distance between my car and the door of that counseling office seemed at least a mile long. After telling the counselor my story, she basically told me that she might not be the person to help me. Once again, my world stopped, and I was stiffened. MS was having a party! My assumptions were right. I should have never tried this! I left crying, and by the time I made it to my car, I was screaming and hollering. *"Why Lord, why? Why Lord, why?"* That's all I could say.

The routine continued: working, teaching, preaching, and helping others. This went on day after day, until one day, *too much* really became too much. I remember driving to work, and about a half mile into my drive, my world really did stop. My body and my muscles literally stopped. I felt like I couldn't breathe. My mind seemed dark. I could hardly think right. I knew something was wrong, so I called my best friend. When she answered the phone, all I could do was scream and cry from the depths of my soul. I was telling her: *"Something is wrong! I don't like how I feel! My mind! My mind! My mind! Help me! My mind!"* Immediately she began to pray in tongues, and eventually told me to pull over. In about ten minutes, she was in my car holding me. I was screaming and crying in the parking lot of a department store. I was about to lose my mind, for real. She told me to call my job and let them know I was not coming in. She then assisted me in getting home. I could barely move. At this point, I knew I had better pull out that insurance list, and find another counselor. I needed help.

After finding another counselor's name, I told the receptionist my story, and again, she made an emergency appointment for me. When I heard the name, I was thinking in my head, *"I believe this is the same counselor my husband and I went to, some years ago."* I later discovered it was the same office, but the previous counselor's wife. I went any way, and that was the best move I had made in a year. I began going to this counselor every week. Every week was a different level of healing. Actually, it made me realize that someone else was operating under the surgical anointing that was similar to mine. Everything she was telling me to do was what I had told others to do. Each session was unique and different. The anointing was powerful, and it was sensed all over the counselor's office. We both sensed what she called "a higher power" in the room, but I understood that we were sensing "the Glory of God." She did not call it the anointing, but I am sure she knew it was something different about our sessions. She taught me a lot, and I am sure the Holy Spirit used me to teach her some things, and bless her as well.

I had gone to her for about three or four months before my husband had come home for a two-week leave. While he was out of the country, most of the time, to my regret, he called me every day. We talked every day! Sometimes we talked two times a day. I hated it! But, I could not tell him. I knew it would take him into a hole of depression that he would not be able to come out of. He was my husband, and I loved him. For about three or four months, I hated hearing his voice, but the love I had for him would not allow me to tell him I did not want to talk to him. Besides, if I did, knowing my husband's stubbornness, he would have never called again, and this would

not have been good for either of us. It would have driven him
into a deeper depression, and I wanted him to stay focused.
I did not want any harm to come to him. Besides, there's no
telling how it would have affected me, if he became too stubborn and angry to call me. When my husband came home,
oddly enough, we had a great time. We agreed to make things
work. But shortly after he returned to his overseas duty station, something happened. I don't know what it was. I just felt
something in the atmosphere. I felt all of the pain and devastating emotions all over again. My trust level was low, so I just
took one day at a time, and pondered on my husband's desires
for us to remain married.

I continued going to my counselor for about 10 months.
Then, suddenly, I just abruptly quit going. I am not sure why,
but I did. Soon afterwards, my husband came back from his
overseas tour, and I wanted to see if he was going to fulfill his
promises of working things out. I wanted to see if all of those
daily telephone calls were going to be justified. I planned a
huge "Home-Coming" celebration for him. It was a big bash! I
spent hundreds of dollars to make it the best celebration ever.
I guess my husband was happy. I was not so sure. Remember,
he was a man who showed me very little, and basically silent
emotions.

I gave him a month, and there were no drastic changes.
There was yet limited compassion, romance, etc. Nevertheless,
I had to "think logically." I had to tell myself, *Muriel, your
husband just came from a war zone. Give the man a break. Let him
readjust.* By this time in our ministry life, we had gained a
new pastor/overseer that my husband had recently met. He
became our pastor/overseer while my husband was out of the
country. I had previously told this new pastor/overseer of our
marriage dilemma, and was eager for him to jump right in
and start some counseling with the both of us. He had promised me while my husband was overseas that he would help us,
upon my husband's return home. I was hoping he would give

us some powerful anointed instructions from Heaven. Well, that did not happen, and I didn't understand why. I waited month after month for our new pastor/overseer to at least have some man-to-man conversations with my husband, just to get to know him. That did not happen. Maybe I was too anxious to get some help. I had been hurting for a long time. Either way, it didn't happen.

Our marriage was like a yo-yo. We were up one week, and down the next. At times conversations were intense. My knowledge of inner-healing let me know that my husband's desire for our marriage to work had to be more than a desire. He needed extensive counseling. After about three months of my husband's return from overseas I gave him the *ultimatum*: *"You get help, or it's over for us. I have given you some time to adjust, but this stuff is crazy! You need help! You haven't paid me any attention! What's wrong with you? Do you really want me, or someone else?"* Evidently he knew I was serious because he agreed to get help, and we went to one counseling session together. The following weekend, we went on what I call, *"Our first real honeymoon."* We went to a local resort and had a wonderful time. My husband talked from his heart, (which he really never did). We aired out a lot of things (everything except a discussion on the infidelity). Overall the trip was great. He told me he would continue counseling weekly, and that he wanted and believed things were going to work for us. In my heart, I was trying to believe everything he had told me, but the clouds of doubt were flooding my mind. Therefore, I began to seek God and do what I had been telling others to do: *Take back what the enemy had stolen from me!* I began to make daily prayer confessions. I allowed the Holy Spirit to take away some of the pain, anguish, and despair that my husband's infidelity had inflicted upon me. The Holy Spirit also took away some of the pain of not receiving compassion and emotional care from my husband.

I don't know when it happened, but I just know it happened. As I daily confessed, change took place in my heart.

You see, my heart had to change in order for change to take place within my husband. We began to talk more. I had previously, (out of anger) told him I would write my life's story and put it in a book. I threatened him, and told him that his infidelity would be a main chapter. Before he left for his overseas tour, he threatened to sue me if I told any of his business to the world. After a few counseling sessions, God changed his heart. He told me to go forth, and write my book, and that he would support me, all the way. He understood that "his business" was also "my business."

Well, as God began to work on the both of us, we both understood that the devil tried to kill our marriage and our lives. We understood that we needed to let the world know that greater is He that is within us, than he that is in the world! God wanted us both to understand that it was our story that was going to give God the Glory! We both understood that we were taking a big step in sharing our testimony with the world, but we also knew that the best was yet to come! Souls would be delivered! Marriages would be restored! And bodies and souls would be healed!

Everything that has taken place during our healing process cannot be put in the pages of a book. However, God has shown me that He will give us opportunities to minister to couples in workshops, seminars, and conferences, all across the world. You see, the rest of my husband's story has yet to be told. This book is about my life, and how God wrapped my pain, in His Glory! I am happy that God did not let the devil kill my baby (promise or promises)! Glory to God! He wrapped my pain in His Glory! Maybe one day God will instruct my husband to put his story in a book. Until then, I have to be the wife, mother, pastor, apostle, professor, friend, counselor, etc. that God has called me to be. I have to daily allow Him to wrap all of my life's pains in His glory, and teach others how to do the same.

Chapter 7

WHAT DO YOU DO WHILE YOU WAIT?

Since my writing of Chapters 5 and 6, a plethora of things occurred within my relationship with God, the church, and within my marriage and family. I accepted the call of God to walk in the office of an Apostle. This time of saying "Yes" to God regarding this call took place while my husband was still out of the country. He knew about it, but understood it more when he arrived home from his tour of duty. The church's school (our largest outreach ministry) grew by leaps and bounds. In a matter of months, we grew from six employees to sixteen. Children were enrolling daily. The rapid expansion was somewhat overwhelming.

As for the church, more covenant Members began to join our ministry. But, something strange was happening. For almost a year and a half of being back from overseas, my husband did not want to do anything in ministry! The ministry was growing, but he wasn't. He basically walked around looking like a zombie. He said his time overseas had caused some mental, physical, and emotional damage to happen within him, and he did not want to be around people. He was constantly telling me that he had Post Traumatic Stress Disorder (PTSD). He said he felt ashamed and embarrassed about what had transpired in our lives and that so many people knew about it. You see, within the time my husband was overseas, the church was going through a healing process, and was eager and ready to accept him as their Co-Pastor, as never before. Many of them knew of our troubles, and they were ready to help my husband by doing whatever it took, to get him into the place he needed to be, in God. Sadly, my husband was still living in the past year's pain. The rest of us had already gone through that level of pain and was walking in a new spiritual level of healing. These times were difficult. When my husband came to church, he would just sit there and stare. There was little to no participation.

The threads in my ribbons of pain began to untie and form a huge bow. History was repeating itself. My husband continued to show no interest in me nor the church. What do you do, while you wait? In my mind, I was saying, *"God you promised me that things would get better. You promised me that you would restore my marriage. You told me if I stayed with my husband, You would make me happy."*

Even though things seemed to have been getting even crazier, suddenly something happened. I remember preaching a message from Acts Chapter 2, and my title was *"And Suddenly."* God used me like never before, to minster to the congregation. Evidently, my husband grabbed a hold of it, because suddenly, he began to work in ministry again. Suddenly, he started reading scriptures during our worship services. Suddenly, he would even pray and expound on the Bible Study lessons. I continued my normal routine of encouraging others, preaching, teaching, counseling, and mending broken hearts. I was also being mother and grandmother. But all the while, my heart was bleeding. Something was still not right, but I couldn't put my hands on it.

Several months later, I noticed changes in my body again. For over six months the pains grew worst by the day. I would drag myself to get into the car to go to the church and preach. After preaching or teaching, I barely made it back to my office before often collapsing on a sofa or chair, and crying, because of the pain in my body. By the time I would make it home, the tears flooded my face, and the pains intensified. I felt like I was dying.

To my surprise, for months my doctor began to re-evaluate my health records. He tested me for some of everything, from cancers to other rare diseases. One day, as I described my pains to my doctor, he noticed something different about my pains. He began to touch various parts of my body, and I wanted to jump out of his office chair when he touched me. It was on this startling visit that he gave me a new diagnosis, Fibromyalgia. Yes, he confirmed that I had both Multiple Sclerosis and Fibromyalgia.

Fibromyalgia varies from one patient to another, but the multiple symptoms it causes are often intertwined. For example, some people do not sleep well and usually struggle with daytime fatigue, difficulty concentrating, depressed mood, and increased pain. I was one of those people who experienced all of those symptoms, most of the time. Another thing about fibromyalgia is the pain. Pain is usually all over the body, and it is severe. My entire body felt like a severe toothache. I could hardly thrive.

Through all of this, I had to continue to wait on the promises of God to be fulfilled. I had to learn what to do *while I was waiting on God*. I pray that the rest of this chapter encourage and bless you, as I explain to you two major things I did while I waited on God. You will see how God wrapped my pain in His Glory, as I consistently did these two things.

First, I had to pray. I know you probably wanted to read something else, but, I don't just mean uttering words. I had to really communicate with God. Communicating with God meant I had to do more than speak words to Him. Often, I had to wait, and listen to what God had to say back to me. Acts 1:14 says, *"These all continued with one accord in prayer and supplication…"* The key word in that scripture is "continued." In order for God to wrap my pain in His Glory, I had to *continue* in prayer. I prayed all the time (at work, at home, at church, in my dreams). Yes, I prayed in my dreams. It was because prayer was not just in my conscious mind. It was also in my subconscious mind. In Acts 1:14, the word 'supplication' comes from the Greek word "Deesis (deh'-ay-sis)." It means a seeking, asking, or an entreating to God. I knew what God had promised me, but I had to stay fervently in prayer in order for me to receive it. I had to keep my petitions before God. Many times, pain will try to force you to stop praying. I make this declaration to you as you read this chapter: *"You will not stop praying! You will be steadfast in prayer, In Jesus' Name!"*

Pain tries to make us forget the importance of prayer. While praying daily, I began to understand more and more that I had to be persistent, like the widow was with the unjust judge (Read Luke 18:2-7). God began to honor my persistent prayer life. When we pray while waiting, we are telling God that we have placed the matter in His hands. In telling Him this, we are not trying to convince Him, but ourselves. And, as you pray, you will find yourself resting in the Glory of God (His Presence). At this point, your pain is now wrapped in God's Glory (His Presence).

Let me take a break and say to you, *"This is not fiction. I teach fiction."* God is real, and His Holy Word is truth. He can take all of your pain and wrap it in His Glory. I am a living witness of this, and I am on a mission for God to let the whole world know that God can wrap your pain in His Glory also.

Now, the second thing I did was study God's Word, day and night. I literally received a "spiritual high" every time I searched the scriptures. I received a "spiritual injection" each time God gave me a new revelation of His Word. The Word of God kept me alive. Hebrews 4:12 says, *" For the word of God is living and powerful, and sharper than any two-edged sword, piercing even to the division of soul and spirit, and of joints and marrow, and is a discerner of the thoughts and intents of the heart."* The Word of God constantly launched me into the presence of God. In His presence, I experienced God's Glory. Each time I was in His presence, God wrapped my pain in His Glory! And as I write this chapter, I am engulfed in His Glory! I believe God right now, that you too are experiencing the Glory of God! I pray that His presence begins to remove your pain. Just stay right there in God's presence. Let God wrap your pain in His Glory! His Glory numbs pain. His Glory removes pain! God's Glory is powerful! His Glory is life-changing!

Chapter 8

FAVORED TO FLOURISH:
YOU WILL RECOVER ALL!

This last chapter is a message of hope. God told me that He will give me double for my trouble! You must believe also, that God is going to give you double, for your trouble. Since God said it, that settles it! The best is yet to come, and you shall recover all! Daily, God has been proving Himself to me, my family, and our church, as being El-Shaddi, the Lord God Almighty. He is truly the God of "more than enough." In my journey to victory, I had to embrace John 10:10. *"The thief cometh not, but for to steal, and to kill, and to destroy: I am come that they might have life, and that they might have it more abundantly."* I had to repeat that scripture, as often as possible. I had to teach and preach that scripture. I also had to mediate on Joel 2:25. *"And I will restore to you the years that the locust hath eaten, the cankerworm, and the caterpillar, and the palmerworm, my great army which I sent among you."*

In this chapter, God has given me an assignment to speak a word of encouragement to you that will change your life forever. Actually, as you read these words, the breath of God will breathe *"life back into you."* The very air where you are will be doused (drenched, saturated, and soaked) with God's Glory. You will sense the presence of God, like never before. As this happens, you will understand what it means for God to wrap your pain in His Glory. I make this declaration to you, with a Holy boldness: *"You Will Recover All!"* God has given me a *"mandate from Heaven,"* to let His people know that *"They shall recover all!"*

Whenever something is taken from you, it leaves a bad taste in your mouth, and a bad feeling within your soul. Sometimes, you want to retaliate, and fight back. Since I had experienced so much pain throughout my life, when the pain of infidelity grabbed me, it put a bad taste in my mouth, not just towards men, but toward people in general. I wanted to fight back! I wanted to make my husband look like an awful person, and pay for cheating on me. I wanted him to be punished, because I had been faithful during our entire marriage. But I had to learn to let God fight for me. God is saying this to you, *right now: "Let me fight for you." And when you do,* "You will recover all!"

Instead of lashing out at my husband and treating him wrongly, each time I came out of God's presence, I felt an even greater love for him. God's Glory taught me that "sin is sin." The Holy Spirit also made me remember how I had told others to forgive, with this same type of dilemma. God taught me how to look at my own flaws and issues. I had to look at the person in the mirror, and focus on getting that person healed. Healed people, heal people. Hence, God's Glory showed me my weak areas. Instead of focusing on my husband's faults, I began to work overtime, fixing my faults. I was determined that the devil was not going to steal and rob me of my joy, nor my marriage. We as believers already know what the devil's job is. I have to keep repeating this throughout this book, to remind you. *"The thief cometh not, but for to steal, and to kill, and to destroy: I am come that they might have life, and that they might have it more abundantly."* (John 10:10) What is it that the thief has stolen from you? Well, get violent and take it back! And take it back, by force!

God spoke to me and told me He had *favored me to flourish*. While I was in my mother's womb, God anointed me to flourish. He did the same for you. I had to realize that other people had experienced some of the same types of pain that I had experienced, but they didn't make it. Many of them lost their minds. Just like me, you too should have lost your mind. You should have been dead. But despite the lies that the devil keeps telling you, you are Highly Favored! God has favored you to flourish!

The word *"flourish"* means *to be strong and healthy*. Flourish also means *to grow well, especially because conditions are right*. I decree and declare that God is making your conditions right to flourish, in Jesus' Name! The devil keeps taunting your mind, telling you that you are not anointed and that you will never grow in God. Yes you will! But if you dwell on what the devil keeps telling you, you will think that you are not favored.

Just like you have read in previous chapters, the thief tried to steal my family. He will do the same thing with your family. He will deceive and trick your spouse, children, or whatever family member he can. He will try to use busy-ness, laziness and crazy-ness to break up homes. He will even try to use so-called friends. A true friend will not be deceptive and false. A true friend will not cause corruption to come to you. A true friend will not cause constant confusion in your life. If that is happening, get those people out of your life, so you can recover all!

As I write this chapter, I am on a Divine Assignment to let you know that you are pregnant with a promise. You need to know the devil will not abort your baby! Remember, when I say 'baby' I am referring to the promise or promises God has given to you. The promise refers to all of the prophetic Words you have ever received. It refers to all of the things God said He was going to do for you, and through you! The devil has tried to discredit your anointing with all of the pain you have experienced. But, I told you, the devil is a liar!

In the natural, once a woman gets pregnant, there is a due date. The devil tried to stop your due date. He wanted to kill your baby! He wanted to kill the promise(s) that God gave to you. But it's too late. If God said a thing, then it is so! He is placing you in the right place, during the right season, and at the right time, and with the right people. That is why the devil tries so hard to steal your fellowship. When you are experiencing pain, fellowship is vital. Don't quit going to church. Don't quit being around God's people.

In all that I was going through in my life, I knew it was vital for me to stay in fellowship with God, and with His people (the church). When we stay in fellowship, God will do what He said He would do in Joel 2:25. *"And I will restore to you the years that the locust hath eaten, the cankerworm, and the caterpillar, and the palmerworm, my great army which I sent among you."* My armor bearers and even my husband did not understand why I would fellowship with other people all the time. I would leave church (after preaching very hard), come home, kick off my shoes, and begin to warm up food that would sometimes feed over 15-20 people. I enjoyed the company. I enjoyed the conversations. I enjoyed the love I felt. I had given out so much love all of my life, and I needed some of the same type of love back. For a while, this happened almost every Sunday. This gave me life! It was a form of therapy for me. You need to discover what type of therapy is good for you. People talked about me for feeding the "church members," but baby, God was wrapping my pain in His Glory, through all of what I was doing. Let people talk. You just do what you need to do, to get healed!

When the devil can make you crawl into your own little box by yourself, he will try to suffocate you. During those times of physical, spiritual, emotional, and mental recovery, I needed fellowship so that I could survive. Being alone would have suffocated me. Don't listen to people who don't understand what God is doing in your life. God's Glory will teach you what to do during your time of spiritual recovery.

Because of sin, many believers have allowed spiritual insects that were mentioned in Joel 2:25 to take things from them. In this book, you have read about the sins that took place in my life. Regardless of the insects (sins) that have tried to take over your life, today God is giving you a "Word of Restoration!" You are favored to flourish, and you will recover all!

If you are grabbing what God is telling you, right now, you might have to place this book aside for a moment and let out a victory shout! This would also be a great time to have a PRAISE BREAK! You are favored to flourish, and you will recover all!

Joel 2:25 did a comparison of four evil spirits of destruction that has moved into many Christian's lives. These evil spirits tried to consume everything I had. They were the: Locusts – *Palmerworms* – *Caterpillars and Cankerworms*. Locusts are well known for their potential of invading crops in swarms of millions, leaving behind devastated fields. Palmerworms are a traveling army of worms. Caterpillars are voracious feeders. When large numbers occur together, they can completely strip the leaves from a tree. Cankerworms are very similar to the worms that were listed above, but is a different color. All of these insects are known destroyers. They would devour everything that was good and decent. That's what the devil tried to do to me. He tried to grab everything that was good and decent in my life, and destroy it. Isn't that what the devil has been trying to do to you? He tried to destroy every good and decent thing in your life.

But, today, you need to get an attitude with the devil and tell him, *"I WANT IT ALL BACK! - "I am Favored to Flourish. I Will Recover All!'* In other words, *"You are recovering all of the stolen property Satan has taken from you!"* In Jesus' Name! Amen and Amen! Let the devil know you are recovering your joy, and declare that you will stop feeling sad and blah all the time. I had to do this! Let the devil know you will recover your love, and you will not harbor hate and bitterness. I had to do this. Declare that you will recover peace, and stress and confusion will have to set up residence elsewhere! Let the devil know that you will recover your marriage and your family. And declare that division, discord, and divorce have to flee from you!

Just as it is in the natural, there is a struggle before the birth. The same is true spiritually. Just before the *"manifestation or birth of the promise,"* there is great warfare. And just before the *"manifestation of the promise,"* the devil will do everything he can to get you to give up, and throw in the towel. Just before your breakthrough you are likely to experience the greatest contradiction to your Promise! But can the Lord encourage you? You just need to get into the right birthing position!

You need to get in whatever birthing position you need to get in, to have your baby. I had to praise God through my pain. I had to literally bless the Lord at all times, and His praises had to continually be in my mouth. I had to make declarations and affirmations to myself daily. I had to encourage myself in the Lord. I had to do more than confess; I had to possess. When you are in the birthing position, this is the most crucial time in your spiritual life. It is the most crucial time in your spiritual life because it is during this time that many promises are aborted!

In my spiritual birthing position, I was reminded of what happened in Exodus 1:19. *"And the midwives said unto Pharaoh, because the Hebrew women are not as the Egyptian women; for they are lively (forceful; powerful) and are delivered ere (beforehand) the midwives come in unto them."* God had to tell me that His promises were not going to be aborted! The Hebrew women were strong, so by the time the cruel Egyptian midwives tried to kill their babies, the babies popped out! Glory to God! Oh, you will give birth! God will fulfill His promises in your life, In Jesus' Name. Amen and Amen! Your baby is about to pop out!

The kingdom of God suffers violence, and the violent must take it by force! You are favored to flourish, and you will recover all! Don't give up on God, and don't give up on yourself. You are stronger than you think. You will recover all!

After years and years of sufferings, troubles, and pain, I truly know how vital it is to have the "Glory" of God in my life. God literally wrapped my pain in His Glory while I was *"in the fire"* of my trials and tribulations. I had to learn that while I was in the fire, the devil was using as many distractions that he could use, to destroy me. I had to learn that God was shifting me to another realm of His Glory. In this book, I have mentioned some of the distractions. There were many more. The pages of a book cannot contain all of them.

During my various trials and tribulations, I had to learn to quit fighting against the fire, and allow God to take me through the fire. Christians must realize that there is victory in the fire! It was in the fire that God kept me wrapped in His Glory. It was in the fire that I preached my greatest sermons. It was in the fire that I taught my best Bible study lessons. It was in the fire that I ministered and prophesied the best!

Fires are issues that cause our spirit man to be arrested and set ablaze with troubles, trials, tribulations, and pain. For those of you who are yet *in the fire*, as you read this chapter, God will bring deliverance to you, and you will feel Him wrapping your pain in His Glory. I decree and declare that you will sense the Glory of God, like never before, even before you finish reading this chapter. *I just prophesied to your future! You are beginning to flourish, right now, in Jesus' Name!*

When trouble, depression, death, pain, anger, and agony taunted me for years, the fire of these situations pushed me further into God's Glory. Fire usually destroys, but my faith, endurance, hope, and aspirations gave me victory in the *fire!* In the midst of chaos--- In the midst of Hell---There was Victory! My faith kept telling me, *"I'm coming out!"* Note that I did not say my *feelings kept telling me this*. My *faith* brought me out. I held on to *my faith*, because I was wrapped in God's Glory.

My faith taught me how to love my husband. Actually, I slowly began to fall in love with him, like no other time before.

As I had been a Spiritual Surgeon to others, God began to use me as a Spiritual Surgeon to bring healing and deliverance to my husband. Day by day, the guilt and shame of his past began to melt away. Day by day, God began to use him. My husband began to understand that God had wrapped my pain in His Glory. He saw me in a totally different way, and I saw him in a totally different way. Even though there were some things I did not like, I loved my husband right where he was.

My testimony is this: *"I am favored to flourish! I will recover all!"* My marriage is flourishing daily. Our communication is better. Our love life is better. Our romance is better. Our relationship with our children is better. The best is yet to come! My husband agreed on the writing of this book, and he has agreed to help others who are experiencing any of the trials and tribulations we went through. Both of us understand that exposure will not be easy, but we also understand that God will wrap any and all of our pain in His Glory.

Today, we have three beautiful grandchildren and a wonderful son-in-law. Our church is growing. Our school is growing. And guess what: "The devil is mad!" If God says a thing, then it is so! II Corinthians 1:20 says, *"For all the promises of God in him are yea, and in him Amen, unto the glory of God by us."* I know God will continue to manifest His promises to us. He will do it "for our good," and "for His Glory."

Finally, if you observe the cover of this book, it is a gift box. God showed me this cover in a vision, and told me what it meant. He told me to get the designer to make a big beautiful red gift box, with a huge yellowish gold ribbon on it, in the shape of a bow. Normally, when a gift is given, most people rush to open it, to see what is inside. There are also times, however, when the wrapping is so pretty that we take our time opening it, so we won't tear the paper. We want to keep it and preserve it for another use.

The red box on the cover is symbolic of the blood of Jesus that was shed on Calvary to wash away our sins. The yellowish gold bow is symbolic of the anointing (the Glory of God). God told me that inside the box was all of my pain that had been wrapped inside His Glory. And He covered the pain with the precious blood of His Son Jesus Christ (the red box). Being the daughter that I am, I had to ask God why he used a gift, because gifts are given to be opened. With that He answered: *"Daughter, you are that beautiful gift box. I have been wrapping your pain in My Glory. My Glory has sustained you. Since I have healed you, unwrap the gift to others. I want to heal others through the pain you have experienced. I want to heal others through your testimonies of My delivering power. You are a vessel of honor and not a vessel of dishonor. Tell your story, daughter. Tell your story, and others will be healed. Tell your story, and others will be blessed. Others need to know how I can wrap their pain in My Glory. Just as the gift box is beautiful, so are you. I have fearfully and wonderfully made you. Others see your beauty, but they also need to see your pain. Tell them how I wrapped your pain in My Glory. Tell the world daughter. Tell them."*

When God initially spoke that to me, it did not totally make sense, but He continued. *"I healed you so you can heal others. Healed people, heal people. Tell others of My healing power. I am the God that healeth thee. I am no respecter of persons. I will heal others through you. The nations are waiting for you. My Glory will sustain you."*

REFERENCES

Brown, Judy. *The Debate and Damage Continue.* God's Word To Women. pp. 2-3. www.godswordtowomen.org/judy-brown. htm.

Don't Forget To Empower Women. Dawn Ministries. http://www. godswodtowomen.org/Yonggi.htm.

Future Church. Cleveland, Ohio, 2001-2003. Info.future-church.org

Grady, Lee. *10 Lies the Church Tells Women.* Lake Mary, Florida: Creation House, 2000.

Grady, Lee. *10 Lies the Church Tells Women.* www.godswordtowomen.org/Lee-Grady.htm.

Holy Bible. King James Version.

Jesus Work Ministry. www.jesusworkministry.com/html/jesus-work- privacy-policy.html

Loughran, David R. *Repairers Of The Breach.* Stewardson, Soctland: Stewarton Bible School, June 1999.

Merrian-Webster. www.merriam-webster.com/dictionary/ online

About The Author

APOSTLE DR. MURIEL AVANT-FUQUA

*A*postle Dr. Muriel Avant Fuqua is both a professor and a pastor who has served in Christian ministry for more than thirty-five years.

She holds a BA and an MA in English Literature and a PhD in Biblical Studies, as well as a Child Development Associate's Degree. She has been an English Professor at Daytona State College since 1989 and was responsible for developing the first African American Literature course at the college.

Stepping into the role of pastor in 2000, Dr. Fuqua went on to accept the mantle of apostleship, becoming officially affirmed and ordained in 2011. She currently serves as the senior pastor of Word and Praise Family Church and the principal of Word and Praise Christian Learning Center. Additionally, she is the founder and overseer of I.N.S.P.I.R.E., a ministry for spiritual covering and partnership.

Married to her co-pastor, Danny Fuqua, they have two children and three grandchildren.

Made in the USA
Columbia, SC
30 August 2023